Adding decimal numbers

KT-214-260

Copy and complete.
Estimate first.

1
```
  T U t
    3·7
+   1·6
_____
```

```
1.    ⑥
    T U t
      3·7
 +    1·6
 _____
      5·3
    1
```

2
```
  T U t
    1·8
+   2·1
_____
```

3
```
  T U t
    2·7
+   4·4
_____
```

4
```
  T U t
    3·4
+   5·8
_____
```

5
```
  T U t
    4·2
+   1·9
_____
```

6
```
  T U t
    5·4
+   6·7
_____
```

7
```
  T U t
    2·8
+   3·2
_____
```

8
```
  T U t
    6·3
+   2·9
_____
```

9
```
  T U t
    4·9
+   3·2
_____
```

10
```
  T U t
    3·7
+   4·2
_____
```

11
```
  T U t
    2·6
+   4·4
_____
```

Each child walks
another 2·8 km.

Write the new totals.

12

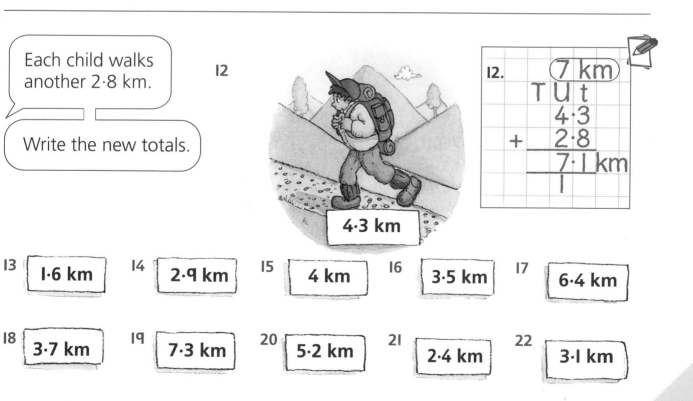

4·3 km

```
12.     ⑦ km
      T U t
        4·3
   +    2·8
   _____
        7·1 km
      1
```

13 1·6 km

14 2·9 km

15 4 km

16 3·5 km

17 6·4 km

18 3·7 km

19 7·3 km

20 5·2 km

21 2·4 km

22 3·1 km

3

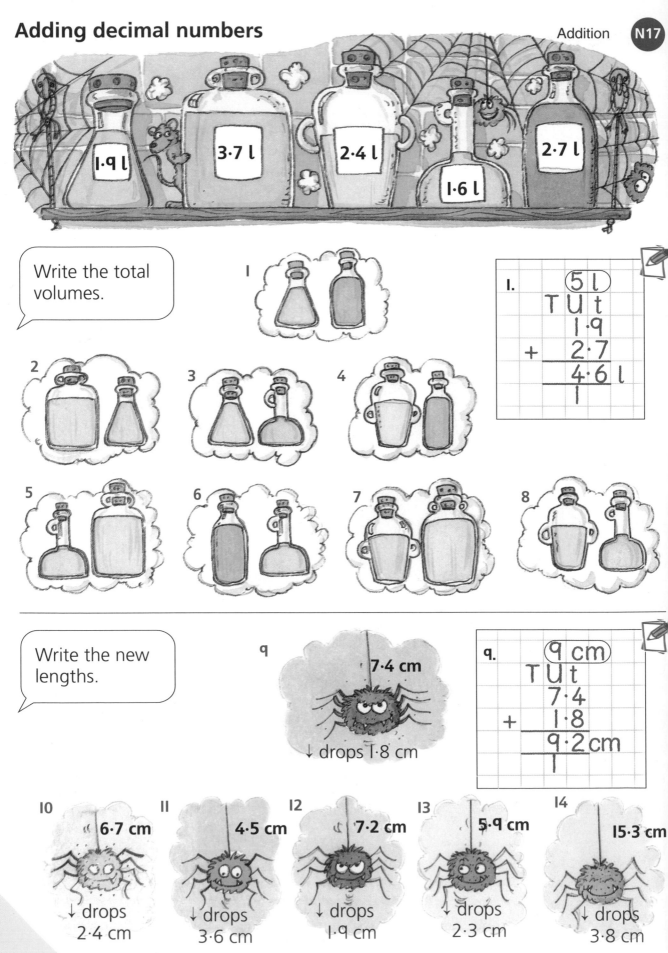

Bottles: 1·9 l, 3·7 l, 2·4 l, 1·6 l, 2·7 l

Write the total volumes.

1.

	5 l	
T	U	t
	1	·9
+	2	·7
	4	·6 l

Write the new lengths.

9 7·4 cm
↓ drops 1·8 cm

9.

	9 cm	
T	U	t
	7	·4
+	1	·8
	9	·2 cm

10 6·7 cm
↓ drops 2·4 cm

11 4·5 cm
↓ drops 3·6 cm

12 7·2 cm
↓ drops 1·9 cm

13 5·9 cm
↓ drops 2·3 cm

14 15·3 cm
↓ drops 3·8 cm

4

Adding decimal numbers

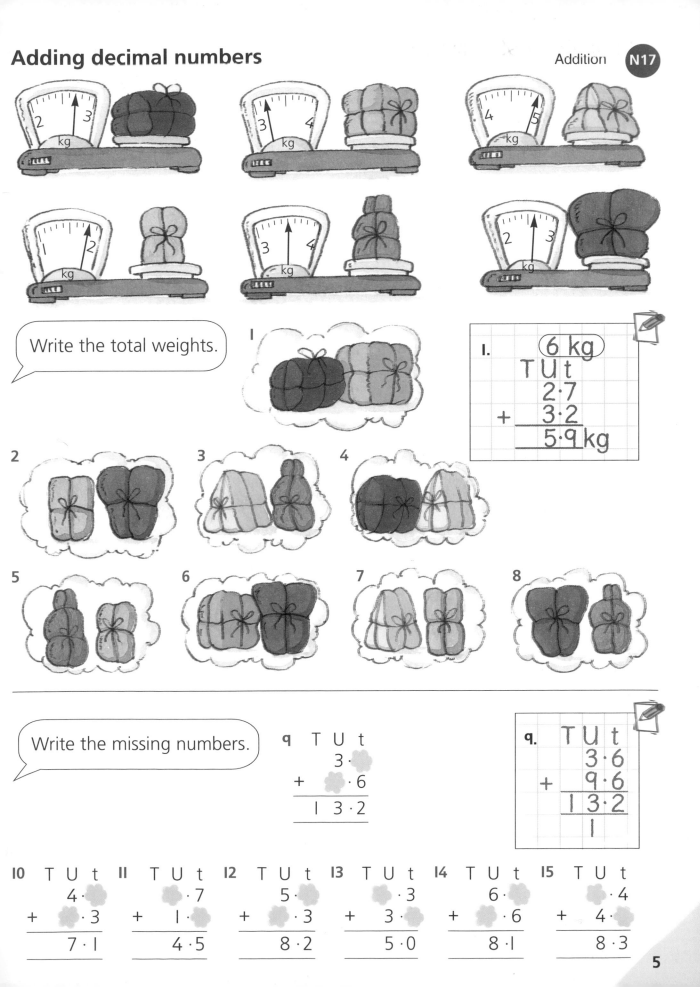

Write the total weights.

1.

	6 kg
	T U t
	2·7
+	3·2
	5·9 kg

9 T U t
    3·
+ ·6
  1 3·2

9.

	T U t
	3·6
+	9·6
	1 3·2
	1

Write the missing numbers.

10	T U t	11	T U t	12	T U t	13	T U t	14	T U t	15	T U t
	4·		·7		5·		·3		6·		·4
+	·3	+	1·	+	·3	+	3·	+	·6	+	4·
	7·1		4·5		8·2		5·0		8·1		8·3

5

Adding decimal numbers

Write the total widths.

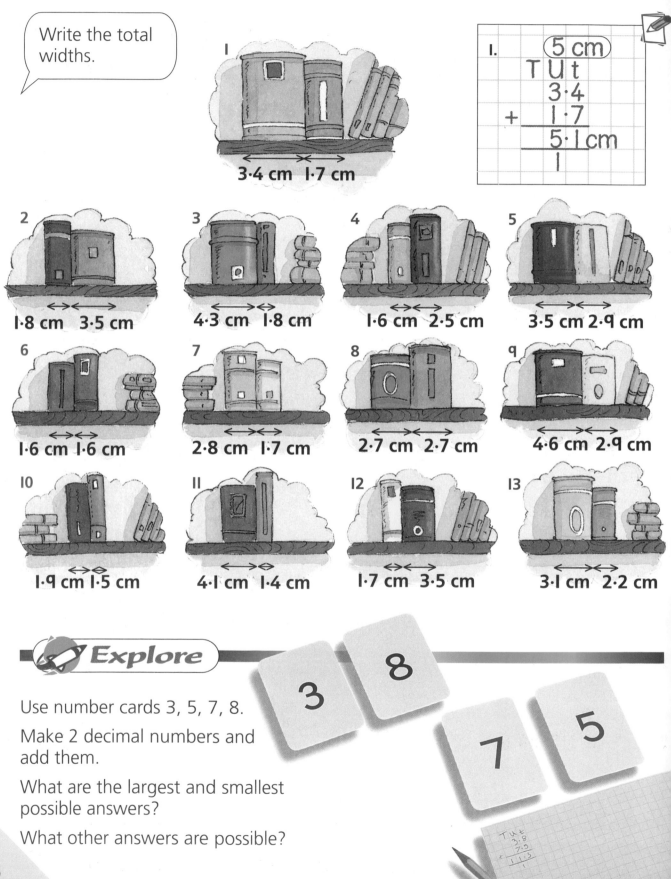

1 3·4 cm 1·7 cm

1.	5 cm
	T U t
	3·4
+	1·7
	5·1 cm
	1

2 1·8 cm 3·5 cm

3 4·3 cm 1·8 cm

4 1·6 cm 2·5 cm

5 3·5 cm 2·9 cm

6 1·6 cm 1·6 cm

7 2·8 cm 1·7 cm

8 2·7 cm 2·7 cm

9 4·6 cm 2·9 cm

10 1·9 cm 1·5 cm

11 4·1 cm 1·4 cm

12 1·7 cm 3·5 cm

13 3·1 cm 2·2 cm

Explore

Use number cards 3, 5, 7, 8.

Make 2 decimal numbers and add them.

What are the largest and smallest possible answers?

What other answers are possible?

Rounding

Write the position of each flag.

Round each number to the nearest thousand.

a. 2 4 0 0
2 4 0 0 → 2 0 0 0

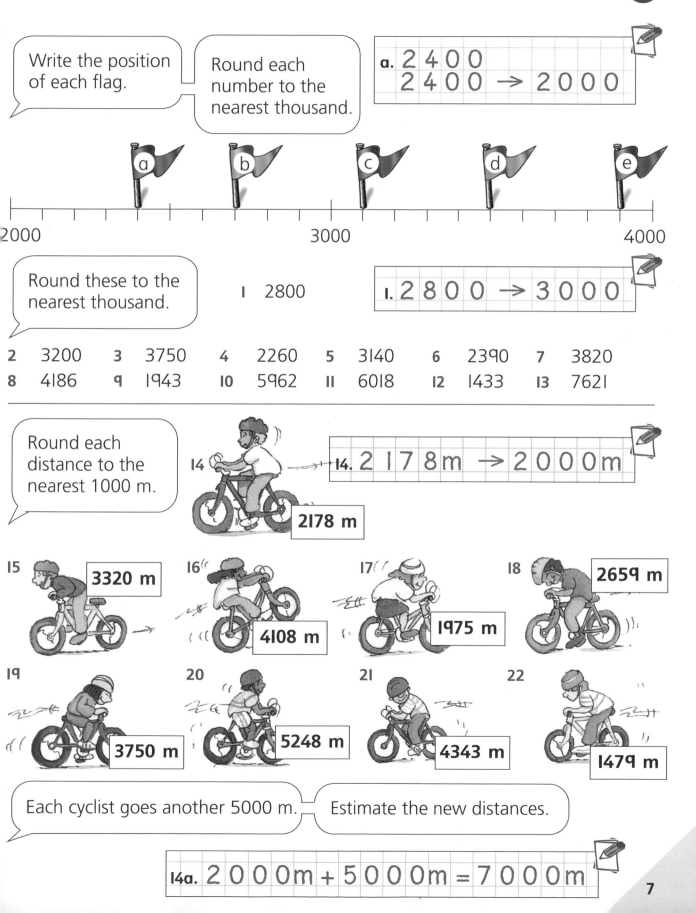

2000   3000   4000

Round these to the nearest thousand.

I   2800

I. 2 8 0 0 → 3 0 0 0

| 2 | 3200 | 3 | 3750 | 4 | 2260 | 5 | 3140 | 6 | 2390 | 7 | 3820 |
| 8 | 4186 | 9 | 1943 | 10 | 5962 | 11 | 6018 | 12 | 1433 | 13 | 7621 |

Round each distance to the nearest 1000 m.

14

14. 2 I 7 8m → 2 0 0 0m

2178 m

15   3320 m

16   4108 m

17   1975 m

18   2659 m

19   3750 m

20   5248 m

21   4343 m

22   1479 m

Each cyclist goes another 5000 m.   Estimate the new distances.

14a. 2 0 0 0m + 5 0 0 0m = 7 0 0 0m

7

Rounding

Choose 2 cars and find the total cost.

£4000 + £3000 = £7000

How many different answers are possible?

Start with one car. Add each of the others, one at a time.

£7000

£3000

£6000

£8000

£4000

Round each number to the nearest thousand, and estimate the total.

Find an exact answer on a calculator.

I. 2462 + 3759
2000 + 4000 = 6000
calculator → 6221

A calculator

1. 2462 + 3759 =

2. 3179 + 2898 =

3. 4428 + 5648 =

4. 6120 + 2039 =

5. 5555 + 2387 =

6. 4071 + 2748 =

7. 3818 + 1659 =

8. 2121 + 2919 =

9. 5031 + 1068 =

10. 7953 + 1234 =

11. 6218 + 3146 =

Rounding

Estimate how much each giant eats in a day.

Find an exact answer on a calculator.

1. $1684\,kg + 2241\,kg$

$2000\,kg + 2000\,kg = 4000\,kg$

calculator → $3925\,kg$

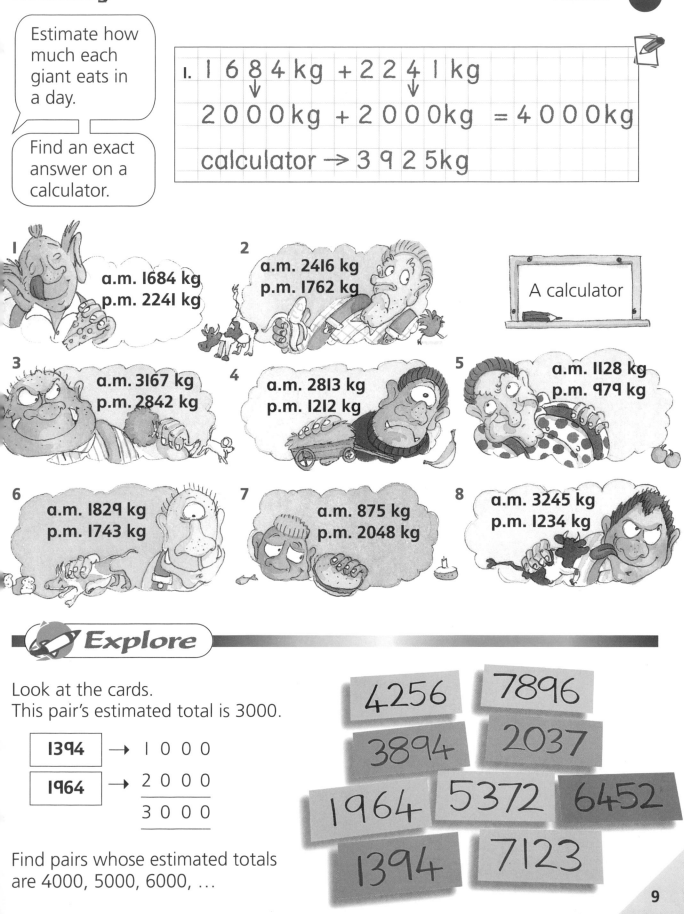

1
a.m. 1684 kg
p.m. 2241 kg

2
a.m. 2416 kg
p.m. 1762 kg

A calculator

3
a.m. 3167 kg
p.m. 2842 kg

4
a.m. 2813 kg
p.m. 1212 kg

5
a.m. 1128 kg
p.m. 979 kg

6
a.m. 1829 kg
p.m. 1743 kg

7
a.m. 875 kg
p.m. 2048 kg

8
a.m. 3245 kg
p.m. 1234 kg

Explore

Look at the cards.
This pair's estimated total is 3000.

1394	→	1 0 0 0
1964	→	2 0 0 0
		3 0 0 0

Find pairs whose estimated totals are 4000, 5000, 6000, …

4256   7896
3894   2037
1964   5372   6452
1394   7123

9

Adding 4-digit numbers

Copy and complete. Estimate first.

1
```
  Th H T U
   4 3 1 6
 + 2 4 8 7
 ─────────
```

1.
```
  ( 6 0 0 0 )
    Th H T U
     4 3 1 6
   + 2 4 8 7
   ─────────
     6 8 0 3
       1 1
```

2
```
  Th H T U
   1 3 4 2
 + 7 0 8 0
 ─────────
```

3
```
  Th H T U
   2 8 1 5
 + 4 9 4 1
 ─────────
```

4
```
  Th H T U
   3 1 8 0
 + 5 6 9 4
 ─────────
```

5
```
  Th H T U
   5 2 7 9
 + 2 7 0 2
 ─────────
```

6
```
  Th H T U
   8 3 0 1
 + 4 1 7 2
 ─────────
```

7
```
  Th H T U
   3 0 1 6
 + 1 9 6 2
 ─────────
```

8
```
  Th H T U
   2 2 9 9
 + 6 8 5 0
 ─────────
```

9
```
  Th H T U
   1 9 6 8
 + 5 1 4 1
 ─────────
```

10
```
  Th H T U
   4 6 3 2
 + 1 1 2 3
 ─────────
```

11
```
  Th H T U
   2 9 2 4
 + 5 3 3 3
 ─────────
```

£1823 is added to each safe.

Write the new amounts.

12 £5132

12.
```
  ( £7 0 0 0 )
     Th H T U
      5 1 3 2
    + 1 8 2 3
    ─────────
    £ 6 9 5 5
```

13 £3148

14 £6243

15 £3780

16 £1814

17 £4891

18 £665

19 £7356

20 £1479

21 £3857

22 £6766

Adding 4-digit numbers

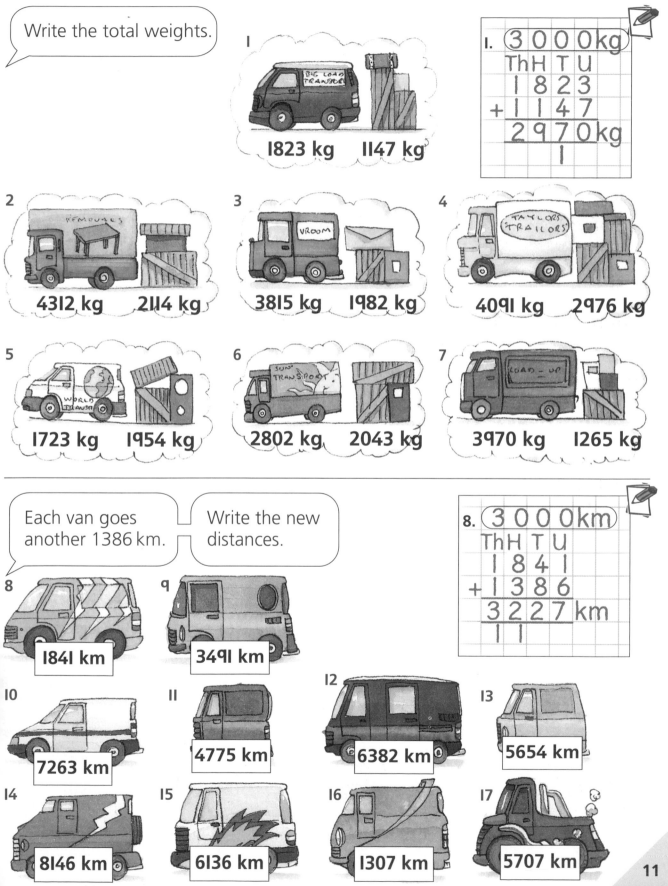

Write the total weights.

1
1823 kg   1147 kg

1. 3 0 0 0 kg
    Th H T U
       1 8 2 3
    + 1 1 4 7
       2 9 7 0 kg
         1

2
4312 kg   2114 kg

3
3815 kg   1982 kg

4
4091 kg   2976 kg

5
1723 kg   1954 kg

6
2802 kg   2043 kg

7
3970 kg   1265 kg

Each van goes another 1386 km.   Write the new distances.

8. 3 0 0 0 km
    Th H T U
       1 8 4 1
    + 1 3 8 6
       3 2 2 7 km
       1 1

8
1841 km

9
3491 km

10
7263 km

11
4775 km

12
6382 km

13
5654 km

14
8146 km

15
6136 km

16
1307 km

17
5707 km

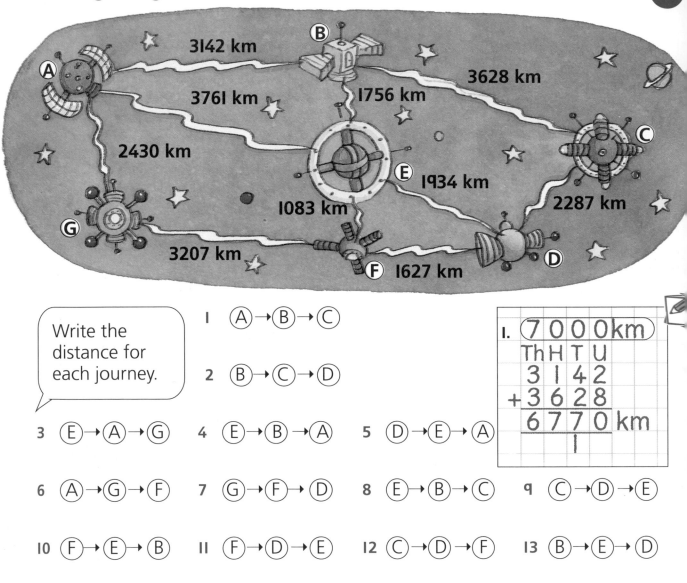

Write the distance for each journey.

1 (A)→(B)→(C)

2 (B)→(C)→(D)

1.	7 0 0 0 km		
	Th H T U		
	3 1 4 2		
+	3 6 2 8		
	6 7 7 0 km		
	1		

3 (E)→(A)→(G) 4 (E)→(B)→(A) 5 (D)→(E)→(A)

6 (A)→(G)→(F) 7 (G)→(F)→(D) 8 (E)→(B)→(C) 9 (C)→(D)→(E)

10 (F)→(E)→(B) 11 (F)→(D)→(E) 12 (C)→(D)→(F) 13 (B)→(E)→(D)

Write the total populations of these space-stations.

Code	Space station	Population
A	Alpha	1148
B	Beetlejuice	1927
C	Canis	3146
D	Delpha	2837
E	Excelsior	4812
F	Fortran	1129
G	Ganymede	3046

14 A and B 15 C and D

16 E and F 17 A and G

18 C and F 19 A and E 20 F and B 21 D and B 22 G and C

Adding 4-digit numbers

Town	Children	Adults
Smilesby	1027	4316
Chucklebury	1123	5620
Laughton	946	3258
Grinville	893	1947
Gleesby	2314	5813
Gigglebridge	2116	6204
Smirk	1245	6732

Write the total populations of these towns.

1 Smilesby

2 Chucklebury   3 Laughton   4 Grinville

5 Gleesby   6 Gigglebridge   7 Smirk

```
1.   5 0 0 0
    Th H T U
     1 0 2 7
   + 4 3 1 6
     5 3 4 3
       1
```

Explore

The total **adult** population of Chucklebury and Grinville is 7567.

Find pairs of towns whose total adult population is:

8151   9071   5205

8679   9936   7574

```
   8 0 0 0
  Th H T U
   5 6 2 0
 + 1 9 4 7
   7 5 6 7
     1
```

13

Write the decimal numbers.

Add to each to make the next whole number.

I. $1.3 + 0.7 = 2.0$

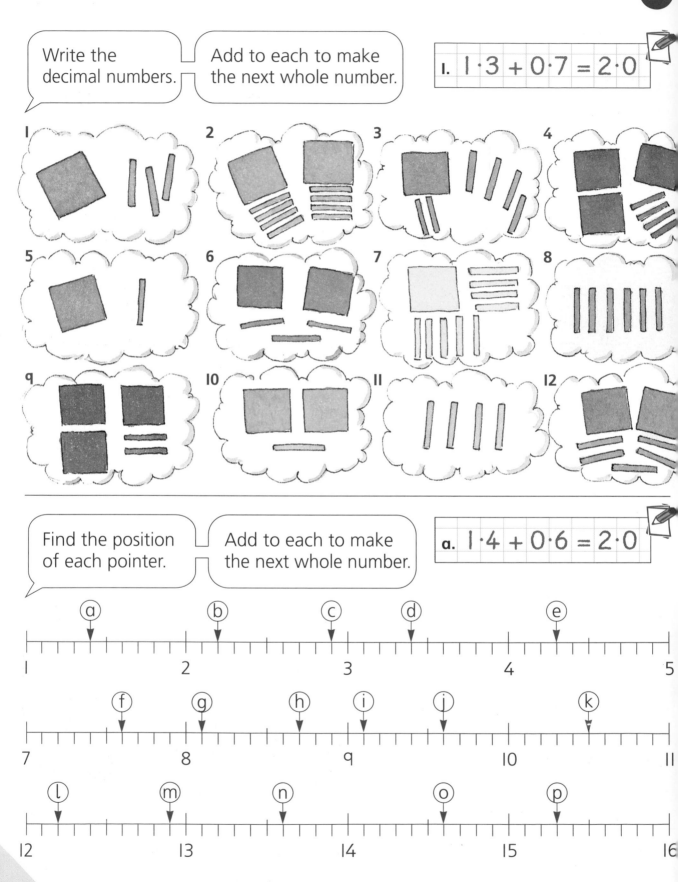

Find the position of each pointer.

Add to each to make the next whole number.

a. $1.4 + 0.6 = 2.0$

The next whole number

Add to each jump to make the next metre.

1. $4{\cdot}2\,m + 0{\cdot}8\,m = 5{\cdot}0\,m$

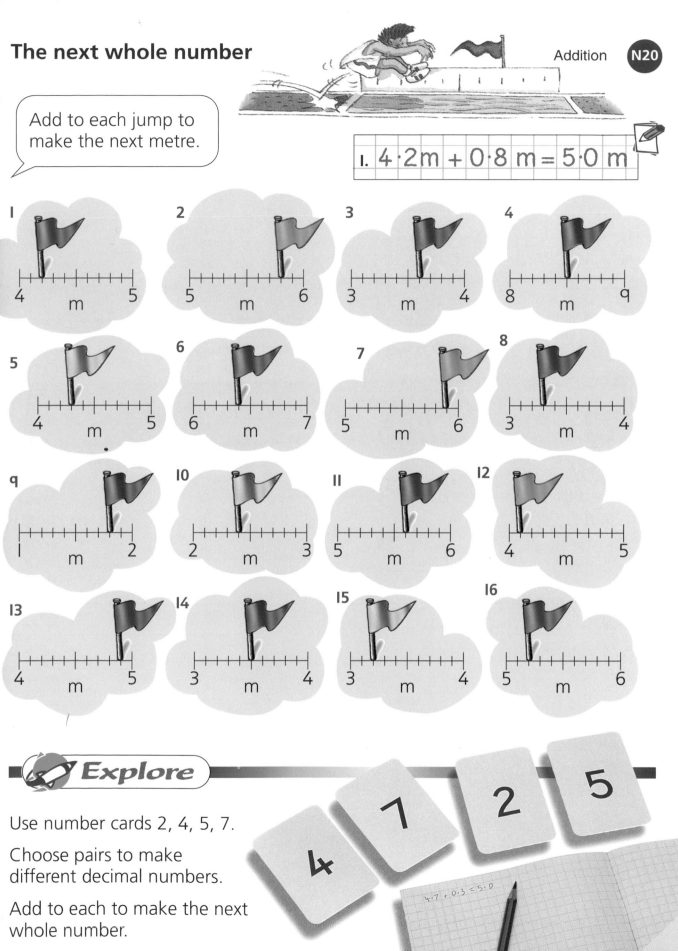

1
4 ——— m ——— 5

2
5 ——— m ——— 6

3
3 ——— m ——— 4

4
8 ——— m ——— 9

5
4 ——— m ——— 5

6
6 ——— m ——— 7

7
5 ——— m ——— 6

8
3 ——— m ——— 4

9
1 ——— m ——— 2

10
2 ——— m ——— 3

11
5 ——— m ——— 6

12
4 ——— m ——— 5

13
4 ——— m ——— 5

14
3 ——— m ——— 4

15
3 ——— m ——— 4

16
5 ——— m ——— 6

Explore

Use number cards 2, 4, 5, 7.

Choose pairs to make different decimal numbers.

Add to each to make the next whole number.

4   7   2   5

$4{\cdot}7 + 0{\cdot}3 = 5{\cdot}0$

The next whole number

Add to each to make the next litre.

I. $2 \cdot 4 l + 0 \cdot 6 l = 3 \cdot 0 l$

2.4 l

2 1·3 l

3 4·9 l

4 5·1 l

5 2·7 l

6 0·3 l

7 1·5 l

8 6·2 l

9 7·4 l

10 0·8 l

11 3·6 l

12 4·2 l

13 5·6 l

Write the missing numbers.

14. $3 \cdot 6 + 0 \cdot 4 = 4 \cdot 0$

14 $+ 0 \cdot 4 = 4 \cdot 0$

15 $+ 0 \cdot 1 = 15 \cdot 0$

16 $+ 0 \cdot 3 = 7 \cdot 0$

17 $+ 0 \cdot 7 = 8 \cdot 0$

18 $+ 0 \cdot 8 = 2 \cdot 0$

19 $+ 0 \cdot 9 = 11 \cdot 0$

20 $+ 0 \cdot 5 = 9 \cdot 0$

21 $+ 0 \cdot 6 = 24 \cdot 0$

22 $+ 0 \cdot 2 = 12 \cdot 0$

23 $+ 0 \cdot 3 = 10 \cdot 0$

24 $+ 0 \cdot 7 = 5 \cdot 0$

25 $+ 0 \cdot 4 = 13 \cdot 0$

Taking away decimal numbers

Copy and complete.
Estimate first.

1
```
  U t
  9·8
- 6·3
------
```

1.   ④
```
  U t
  9·8
- 6·3
------
  3·5
```

2
```
  U t
  4·7
- 2·1
------
```

3
```
  U t
  6·5
- 3·4
------
```

4
```
  U t
  9·7
- 6·2
------
```

5
```
  U t
  3·4
- 1·3
------
```

6
```
  U t
  6·5
- 4·1
------
```

7
```
  U t
  8·3
- 5·2
------
```

8
```
  U t
  2·6
- 1·5
------
```

9
```
  U t
  7·2
- 3·1
------
```

10
```
  U t
  9·8
- 5·6
------
```

11
```
  U t
  5·7
- 2·2
------
```

Each barrel leaks 1·4 l.

Write how much is left.

12 4·8 l

12.   ④ l
```
  U t
  4·8
- 1·4
------
  3·4 l
```

13 9·6 l

14 8·7 l

15 7·9 l

16 9·5 l

17 6·7 l

18 5·6 l

19 6·6 l

20 9·7 l

21 2·8 l

22 3·6 l

Taking away decimal numbers

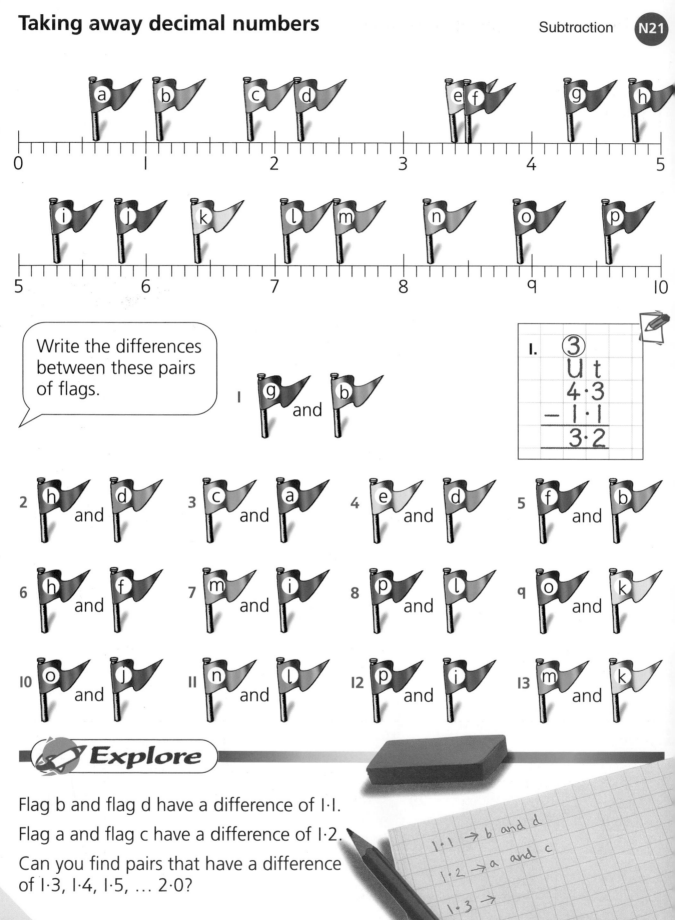

Write the differences between these pairs of flags.

1 g and b

1.
```
    U  t
    4 · 3
 -  1 · 1
 ───────
    3 · 2
```

2 h and d

3 c and a

4 e and d

5 f and b

6 h and f

7 m and i

8 p and l

9 o and k

10 o and j

11 n and l

12 p and i

13 m and k

Explore

Flag b and flag d have a difference of 1·1.

Flag a and flag c have a difference of 1·2.

Can you find pairs that have a difference of 1·3, 1·4, 1·5, ... 2·0?

1·1 → b and d
1·2 → a and c
1·3 →

Taking away decimal numbers

Write the missing widths.

1

3·4 m
8·7 m

1.	(6m)	
	U	t
	8·	7
−	3·	4
	5·	3 m

2

6·5 m
9·8 m

3

4·2 m
6·4 m

4

5·1 m
7·9 m

5

2·3 m
5·3 m

6

1·6 m
4·7 m

7

5·3 m
8·8 m

8

6·1 m
9·4 m

q

1·4 m
5·6 m

10

4·5 m
7·7 m

Take each blue number away from each red number.

9·6   7·8

2·4

3·1   4·3   8·5

II.	(7)	
	U	t
	9·	6
−	3·	1
	6·	5

Taking away decimal numbers

Write the missing weights.

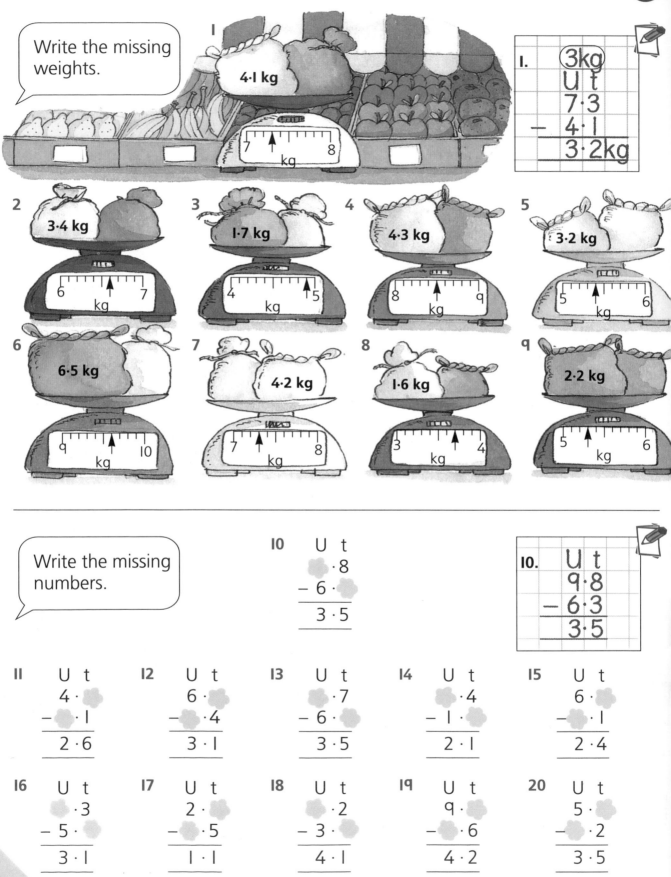

I 4·1 kg

```
I.    3kg
      U t
      7·3
    − 4·1
      3·2kg
```

2 3·4 kg

3 1·7 kg

4 4·3 kg

5 3·2 kg

6 6·5 kg

7 4·2 kg

8 1·6 kg

9 2·2 kg

Write the missing numbers.

```
10    U t
       ·8
    − 6·
      3·5
```

```
10.   U t
      9·8
    − 6·3
      3·5
```

```
11    U t        12    U t        13    U t        14    U t        15    U t
      4·               6·               ·7               ·4               6·
    −   ·1           −   ·4         − 6·             − 1·             −   ·1
      2·6              3·1              3·5              2·1              2·4
```

```
16    U t        17    U t        18    U t        19    U t        20    U t
       ·3               2·               ·2               9·               5·
    − 5·             −   ·5         − 3·             −   ·6           −   ·2
      3·1              1·1              4·1              4·2              3·5
```

20

Taking away decimal numbers

Copy and complete.

1
```
  U t
  7·2
- 4·8
─────
```

1.
```
   U t      +0·2      U t
   7·2                7·4
 - 4·8              - 5·0
                    ─────
                     2·4
```

2
```
  U t
  6·4
- 3·8
─────
```

3
```
  U t
  7·5
- 5·8
─────
```

4
```
  U t
  8·3
- 2·5
─────
```

5
```
  U t
  9·6
- 3·9
─────
```

6
```
  U t
  6·4
- 1·7
─────
```

7
```
  U t
  5·1
- 0·4
─────
```

8
```
  U t
  4·2
- 2·6
─────
```

9
```
  U t
  8·0
- 7·2
─────
```

10
```
  U t
  5·5
- 1·9
─────
```

11
```
  U t
  5·0
- 4·7
─────
```

Write how much ice-cream is left.

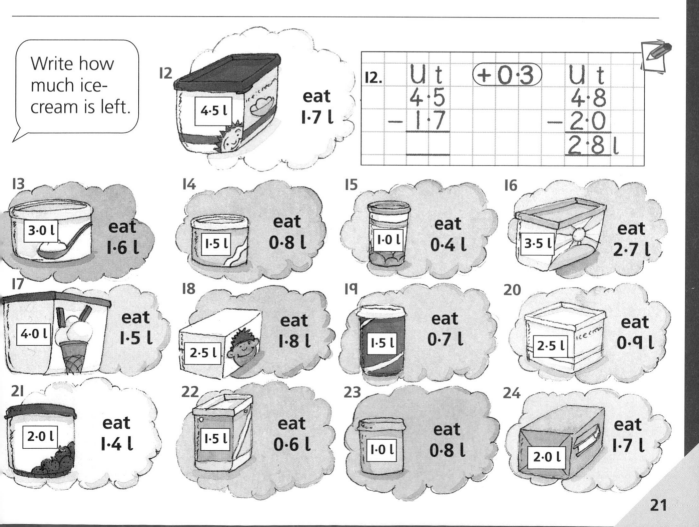

12 4·5 l — eat 1·7 l

12.
```
   U t      +0·3      U t
   4·5                4·8
 - 1·7              - 2·0
                    ─────
                     2·8 l
```

13 3·0 l — eat 1·6 l

14 1·5 l — eat 0·8 l

15 1·0 l — eat 0·4 l

16 3·5 l — eat 2·7 l

17 4·0 l — eat 1·5 l

18 2·5 l — eat 1·8 l

19 1·5 l — eat 0·7 l

20 2·5 l — eat 0·9 l

21 2·0 l — eat 1·4 l

22 1·5 l — eat 0·6 l

23 1·0 l — eat 0·8 l

24 2·0 l — eat 1·7 l

Copy and complete.

1
```
  U  t
  7 · 2
- 4 · 8
───────
```

```
1.   U  t
    ⁶7·¹2
   - 4·8
   ──────
     2·4
```

2
```
  U  t
  6 · 4
- 3 · 8
───────
```

3
```
  U  t
  7 · 5
- 5 · 8
───────
```

4
```
  U  t
  8 · 3
- 2 · 5
───────
```

5
```
  U  t
  9 · 6
- 3 · 9
───────
```

6
```
  U  t
  6 · 4
- 1 · 7
───────
```

7
```
  U  t
  5 · 1
- 0 · 4
───────
```

8
```
  U  t
  4 · 2
- 2 · 6
───────
```

9
```
  U  t
  8 · 0
- 7 · 2
───────
```

10
```
  U  t
  5 · 5
- 1 · 9
───────
```

11
```
  U  t
  5 · 0
- 4 · 7
───────
```

Write how much ice-cream is left.

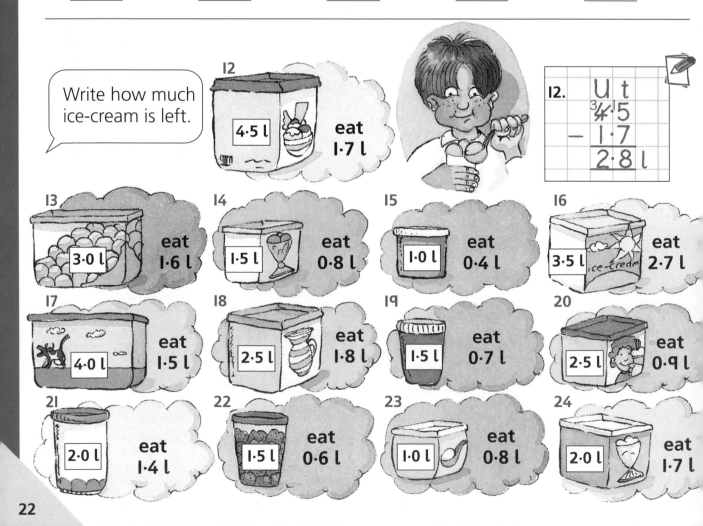

12 4·5 l   eat 1·7 l

```
12.   U  t
     ³4·5
    - 1·7
    ──────
      2·8 l
```

13 3·0 l   eat 1·6 l

14 1·5 l   eat 0·8 l

15 1·0 l   eat 0·4 l

16 3·5 l   eat 2·7 l

17 4·0 l   eat 1·5 l

18 2·5 l   eat 1·8 l

19 1·5 l   eat 0·7 l

20 2·5 l   eat 0·9 l

21 2·0 l   eat 1·4 l

22 1·5 l   eat 0·6 l

23 1·0 l   eat 0·8 l

24 2·0 l   eat 1·7 l

22

Taking away decimal numbers

The sleeping-bags are taken off.

Write the new weights.

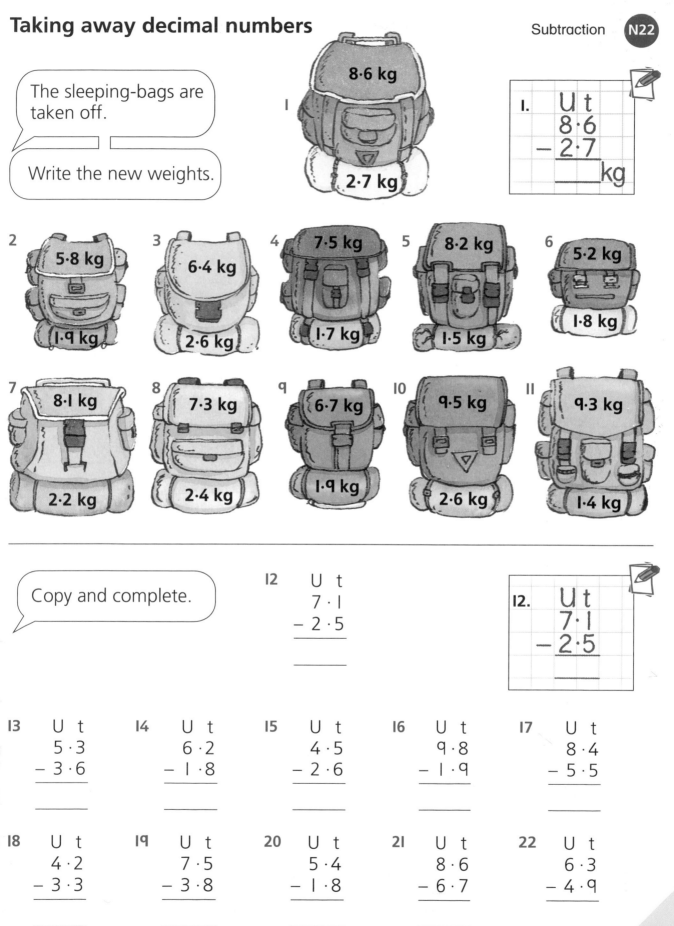

1   8·6 kg

2·7 kg

1.
```
U t
8·6
− 2·7
        kg
```

2   5·8 kg
1·9 kg

3   6·4 kg
2·6 kg

4   7·5 kg
1·7 kg

5   8·2 kg
1·5 kg

6   5·2 kg
1·8 kg

7   8·1 kg
2·2 kg

8   7·3 kg
2·4 kg

q   6·7 kg
1·9 kg

10   9·5 kg
2·6 kg

11   9·3 kg
1·4 kg

Copy and complete.

12
```
U t
7 · 1
− 2 · 5
```

12.
```
U t
7·1
− 2·5
```

13
```
U t
5 · 3
− 3 · 6
```

14
```
U t
6 · 2
− 1 · 8
```

15
```
U t
4 · 5
− 2 · 6
```

16
```
U t
9 · 8
− 1 · 9
```

17
```
U t
8 · 4
− 5 · 5
```

18
```
U t
4 · 2
− 3 · 3
```

19
```
U t
7 · 5
− 3 · 8
```

20
```
U t
5 · 4
− 1 · 8
```

21
```
U t
8 · 6
− 6 · 7
```

22
```
U t
6 · 3
− 4 · 9
```

Taking away decimal numbers

Write the new weights.

eats 1·5 kg

7·3 kg

1.
```
   U t
   7·3
 − 1·5
 _____ kg
```

2. 5·2 kg — eats 1·4 kg

3. 1·3 kg — eats 0·8 kg

4. 4·1 kg — eats 2·2 kg

5. 5·5 kg — eats 1·8 kg

6. 2·4 kg — eats 0·9 kg

7. 8·5 kg — eats 2·7 kg

8. 7·3 kg — eats 3·5 kg

9. 6·4 kg — eats 1·9 kg

10. 3·5 kg — eats 1·7 kg

11. 6·3 kg — eats 1·5 kg

12. 7·4 kg — eats 2·6 kg

13. 4·4 kg — eats 3·8 kg

Choose 4 balloons and make 2 different decimal numbers.

Take the smaller from the larger.

Do this 10 times.

14.
```
   U t
   5·8
 − 2·3
 _____
   3·5
```

5 2 3 8 1

Use number cards to help you.

24

Taking away decimal numbers

Copy and complete.

1
```
  T U t
  1 7·3
- 1 4·5
```

```
1.  T U t
    1 7·3
  - 1 4·5
```

2
```
  T U t
  1 6·2
- 1 2·5
```

3
```
  T U t
  1 4·3
- 1 1·8
```

4
```
  T U t
  1 8·4
- 1 4·9
```

5
```
  T U t
  1 2·5
- 1 0·6
```

6
```
  T U t
  2 2·4
- 1 1·8
```

7
```
  T U t
  2 8·3
- 1 5·9
```

8
```
  T U t
  3 8·1
-   7·4
```

9
```
  T U t
  4 9·2
- 3 2·5
```

10
```
  T U t
  5 8·5
- 2 6·8
```

11
```
  T U t
  1 9·7
-   4·9
```

Write the new heights.

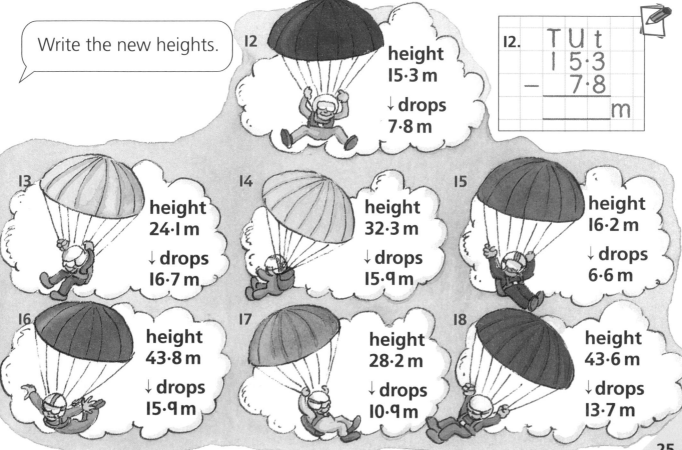

12
height
15·3 m
↓ drops
7·8 m

```
12.  T U t
     1 5·3
   -   7·8
          m
```

13
height
24·1 m
↓ drops
16·7 m

14
height
32·3 m
↓ drops
15·9 m

15
height
16·2 m
↓ drops
6·6 m

16
height
43·8 m
↓ drops
15·9 m

17
height
28·2 m
↓ drops
10·9 m

18
height
43·6 m
↓ drops
13·7 m

25

Halves and quarters

Write one half of each number.

1 16 cubes

1. $\frac{1}{2}$ of 1 6 = 8

2 22 cubes

3 30 cubes

4 28 cubes

Use cubes to help you.

5 24 cubes

6 12 cubes

7 18 cubes

8 32 cubes

Write one quarter of each amount.

9 40p

9. $\frac{1}{4}$ of 4 0p = 1 0p

10 20p

11 60p

12 32p

Use coins to help you.

13 36p

14 16p

15 64p

16 80p

17 24p

18 44p

19 28p

20 48p

Fractions

Write one third of each number.

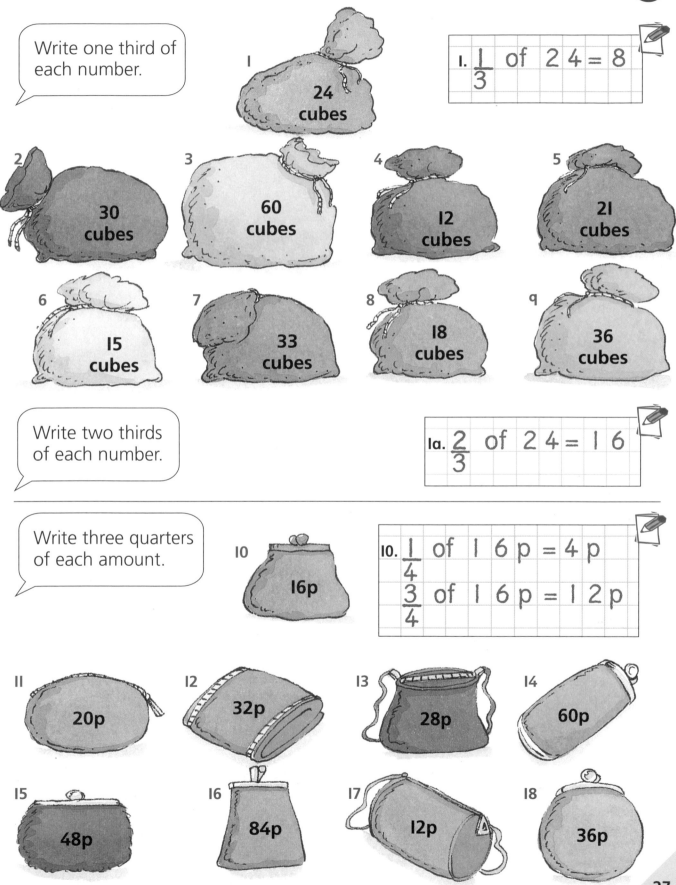

1 24 cubes

1. $\frac{1}{3}$ of 2 4 = 8

2 30 cubes

3 60 cubes

4 12 cubes

5 21 cubes

6 15 cubes

7 33 cubes

8 18 cubes

9 36 cubes

Write two thirds of each number.

1a. $\frac{2}{3}$ of 2 4 = 1 6

Write three quarters of each amount.

10 16p

10. $\frac{1}{4}$ of 1 6 p = 4 p

$\frac{3}{4}$ of 1 6 p = 1 2 p

11 20p

12 32p

13 28p

14 60p

15 48p

16 84p

17 12p

18 36p

27

Fractions

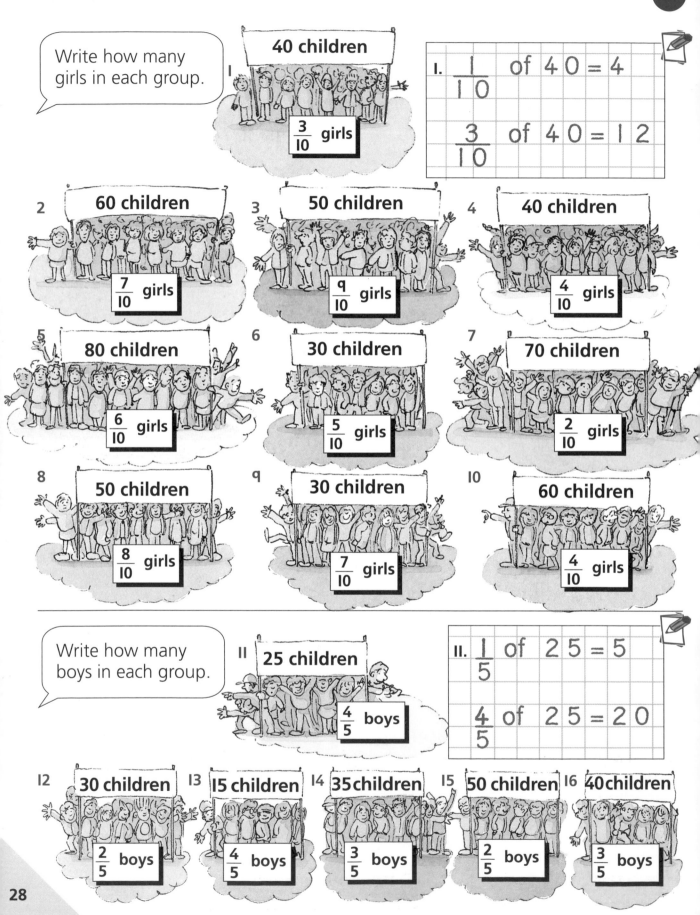

Write how many girls in each group.

40 children
$\frac{3}{10}$ girls

I. $\frac{1}{10}$ of 40 = 4

$\frac{3}{10}$ of 40 = 12

2 60 children — $\frac{7}{10}$ girls

3 50 children — $\frac{9}{10}$ girls

4 40 children — $\frac{4}{10}$ girls

5 80 children — $\frac{6}{10}$ girls

6 30 children — $\frac{5}{10}$ girls

7 70 children — $\frac{2}{10}$ girls

8 50 children — $\frac{8}{10}$ girls

9 30 children — $\frac{7}{10}$ girls

10 60 children — $\frac{4}{10}$ girls

Write how many boys in each group.

11 25 children — $\frac{4}{5}$ boys

II. $\frac{1}{5}$ of 25 = 5

$\frac{4}{5}$ of 25 = 20

12 30 children — $\frac{2}{5}$ boys

13 15 children — $\frac{4}{5}$ boys

14 35 children — $\frac{3}{5}$ boys

15 50 children — $\frac{2}{5}$ boys

16 40 children — $\frac{3}{5}$ boys

Fractions

> Write how many minutes.

1 $\frac{3}{4}$ of an hour

I. $\frac{3}{4}$ of 60 = 45 minutes

2 $\frac{3}{5}$ of an hour

3 $\frac{2}{3}$ of an hour

4 $\frac{1}{6}$ of an hour

5 $\frac{2}{5}$ of an hour

6 $\frac{5}{6}$ of an hour

7 $\frac{3}{10}$ of an hour

8 $\frac{2}{6}$ of an hour

9 $\frac{7}{10}$ of an hour

10 $\frac{4}{5}$ of an hour

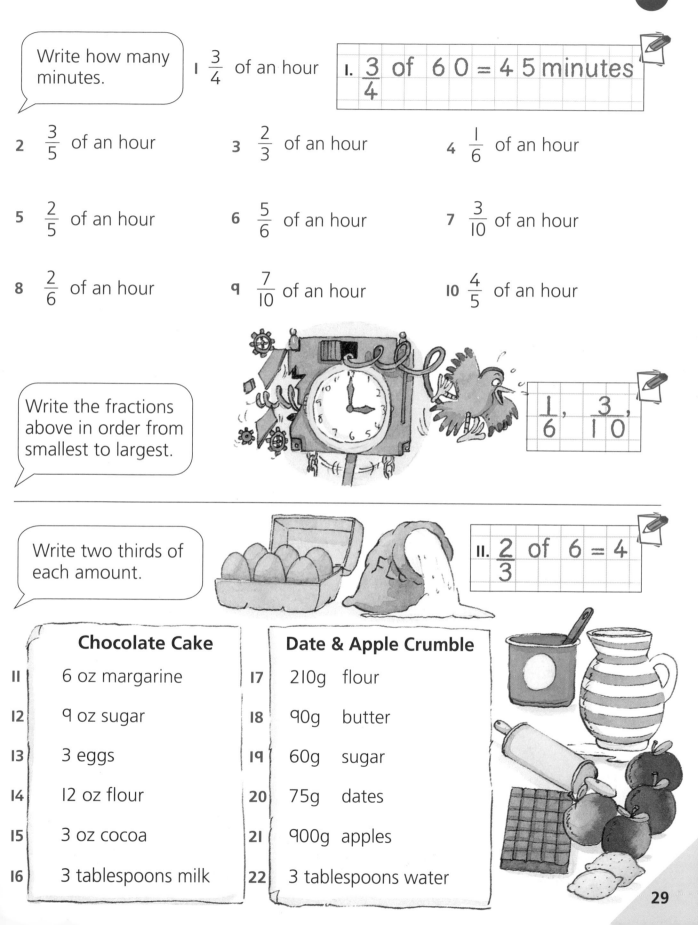

> Write the fractions above in order from smallest to largest.

$\frac{1}{6}$, $\frac{3}{10}$,

> Write two thirds of each amount.

II. $\frac{2}{3}$ of 6 = 4

Chocolate Cake

11 6 oz margarine

12 9 oz sugar

13 3 eggs

14 12 oz flour

15 3 oz cocoa

16 3 tablespoons milk

Date & Apple Crumble

17 210g flour

18 90g butter

19 60g sugar

20 75g dates

21 900g apples

22 3 tablespoons water

Copy and complete.

1 $\frac{2}{5}$ of 20 =

1. $\frac{1}{5}$ of 20 = 4

   $\frac{2}{5}$ of 20 = 8

2 $\frac{2}{3}$ of 27 =

3 $\frac{4}{5}$ of 20 =

4 $\frac{3}{5}$ of 25 =

5 $\frac{3}{4}$ of 32 =

6 $\frac{3}{8}$ of 16 =

7 $\frac{2}{7}$ of 14 =

8 $\frac{7}{8}$ of 24 =

9 $\frac{5}{6}$ of 36 =

10 $\frac{5}{8}$ of 40 =

11 $\frac{2}{3}$ of 66 =

12 $\frac{4}{5}$ of 40 =

13 $\frac{3}{4}$ of 48 =

14 $\frac{3}{8}$ of 32 =

15 $\frac{5}{6}$ of 48 =

16 $\frac{3}{7}$ of 21 =

Write how much each child spends.

17. $\frac{1}{4}$ of 100p = 25p

    $\frac{3}{4}$ of 100p = 75p

17 £1 spends $\frac{3}{4}$

18 £1 spends $\frac{1}{4}$

19 £1 spends $\frac{2}{5}$

20 £1 spends $\frac{3}{10}$

21 £1 spends $\frac{4}{5}$

Equivalent fractions

Write the fraction of each grid that is blue.

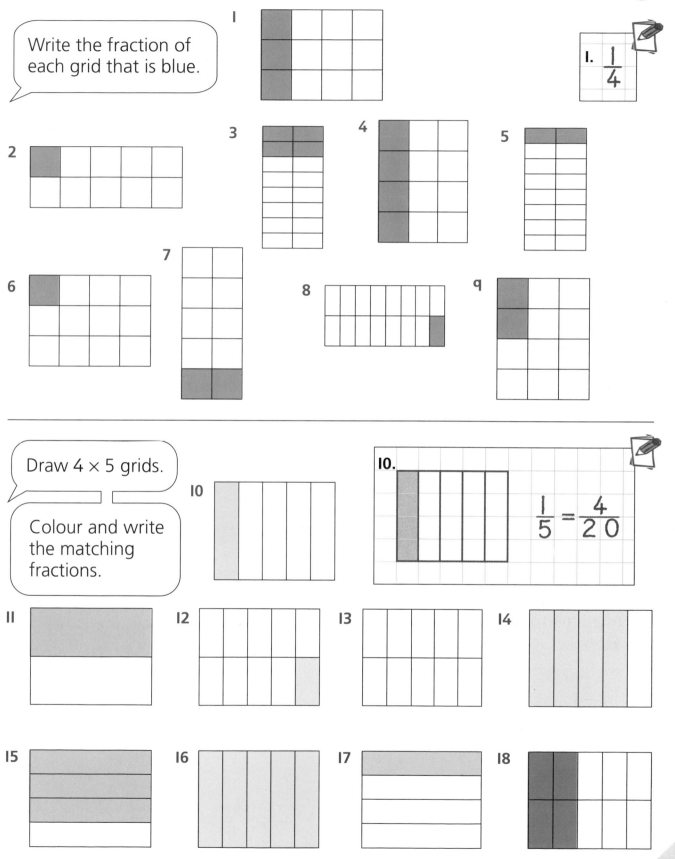

I. $\dfrac{1}{4}$

Draw 4 × 5 grids.

Colour and write the matching fractions.

10. $\dfrac{1}{5} = \dfrac{4}{20}$

Equivalent fractions

Write pairs of fractions that match.

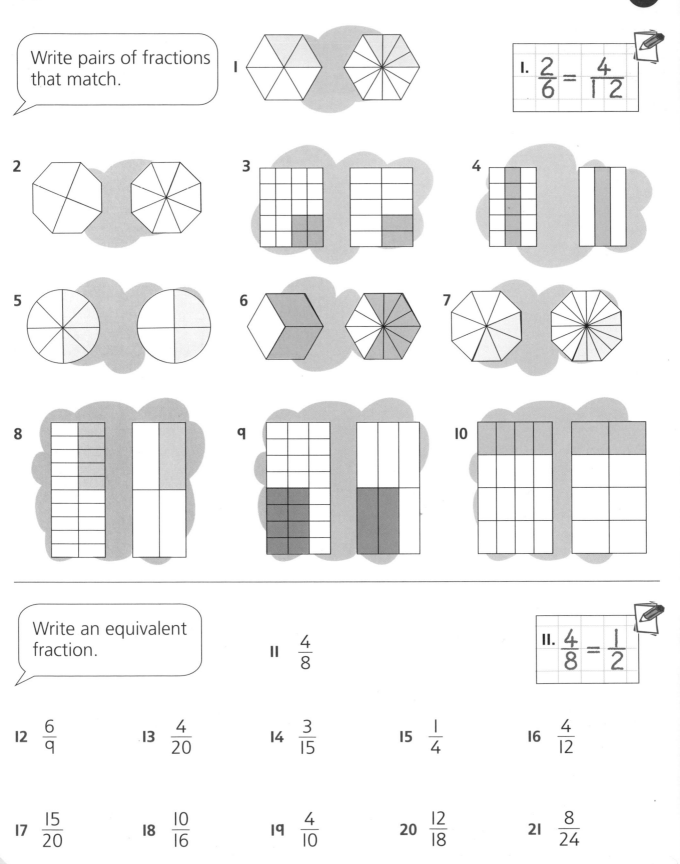

I. $\dfrac{2}{6} = \dfrac{4}{12}$

1

2

3

4

5

6

7

8

9

10

Write an equivalent fraction.

II $\dfrac{4}{8}$

II. $\dfrac{4}{8} = \dfrac{1}{2}$

12 $\dfrac{6}{9}$

13 $\dfrac{4}{20}$

14 $\dfrac{3}{15}$

15 $\dfrac{1}{4}$

16 $\dfrac{4}{12}$

17 $\dfrac{15}{20}$

18 $\dfrac{10}{16}$

19 $\dfrac{4}{10}$

20 $\dfrac{12}{18}$

21 $\dfrac{8}{24}$

Equivalent fractions

Write the missing number.

1   $\dfrac{1}{} = \dfrac{8}{16}$

> I. $\dfrac{1}{2} = \dfrac{8}{16}$

2   $\dfrac{3}{9} = \dfrac{}{3}$

3   $\dfrac{3}{10} = \dfrac{6}{}$

4   $\dfrac{}{36} = \dfrac{5}{12}$

5   $\dfrac{6}{9} = \dfrac{12}{}$

6   $\dfrac{8}{24} = \dfrac{4}{}$

7   $\dfrac{6}{8} = \dfrac{}{24}$

8   $\dfrac{2}{5} = \dfrac{}{10}$

9   $\dfrac{2}{} = \dfrac{4}{12}$

10   $\dfrac{1}{3} = \dfrac{}{15}$

There are 36 sweets in a box.

Write how many sweets each child gets.

> II. $\dfrac{1}{3}$ of 3 6 = 1 2

11   Amit, $\dfrac{1}{3}$

12   Uma, $\dfrac{3}{4}$

13   Linda, $\dfrac{6}{12}$

14   Kim, $\dfrac{9}{12}$

15   Sue, $\dfrac{5}{6}$

16   Tom, $\dfrac{4}{6}$

17   Simon, $\dfrac{3}{12}$

18   David, $\dfrac{8}{12}$

19   Sujata, $\dfrac{10}{12}$

20   Arun, $\dfrac{3}{6}$

21   Kate, $\dfrac{3}{9}$

22   Jim, $\dfrac{1}{4}$

Which pairs get the same number of sweets?

> Amit and Kate $\dfrac{1}{3} = \dfrac{3}{9}$

Write sets of
equivalent fractions.

1. $\dfrac{3}{4} = \dfrac{6}{8} = \dfrac{9}{12}$

$\dfrac{6}{8}$

$\dfrac{13}{16}$

$\dfrac{3}{5}$

$\dfrac{10}{24}$

$\dfrac{26}{32}$

$\dfrac{8}{16}$

$\dfrac{3}{8}$

$\dfrac{2}{5}$

$\dfrac{3}{4}$

$\dfrac{9}{15}$

$\dfrac{1}{2}$

$\dfrac{4}{12}$

$\dfrac{3}{6}$

$\dfrac{1}{3}$

$\dfrac{5}{12}$

$\dfrac{4}{10}$

$\dfrac{9}{12}$

Write the first 6
members of each set.

9. $\dfrac{1}{2} = \dfrac{2}{4} = \dfrac{3}{6} =$

9 $\dfrac{1}{2}$

10 $\dfrac{2}{3}$

11 $\dfrac{3}{4}$

12 $\dfrac{2}{5}$

Tenths

Write each number as a fraction and a decimal.

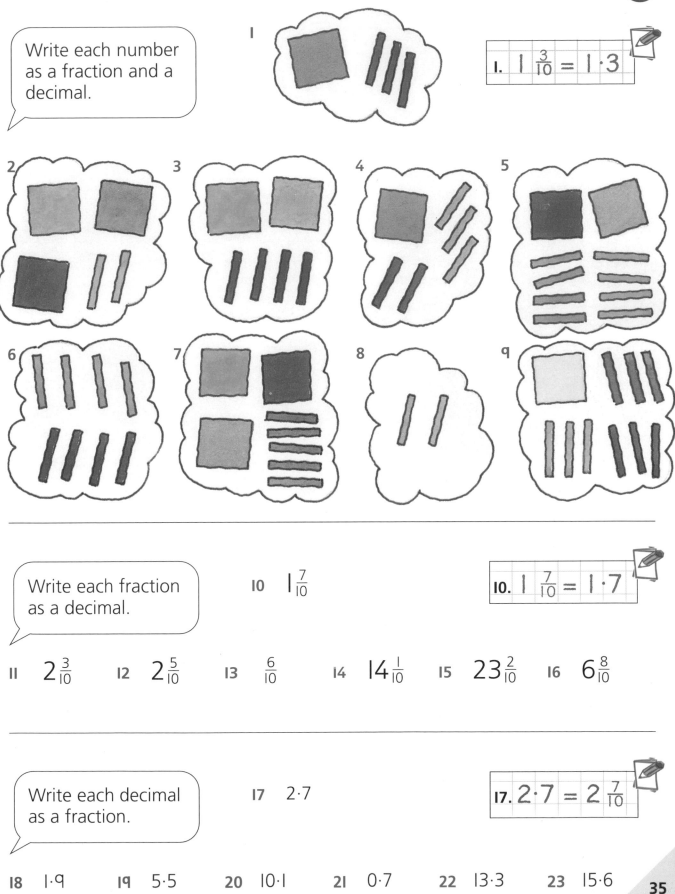

1.

1. $1\frac{3}{10} = 1 \cdot 3$

2

3

4

5

6

7

8

9

Write each fraction as a decimal.

10   $1\frac{7}{10}$

10. $1\frac{7}{10} = 1 \cdot 7$

11   $2\frac{3}{10}$ 12 $2\frac{5}{10}$ 13 $\frac{6}{10}$ 14 $14\frac{1}{10}$ 15 $23\frac{2}{10}$ 16 $6\frac{8}{10}$

Write each decimal as a fraction.

17   $2 \cdot 7$

17. $2 \cdot 7 = 2\frac{7}{10}$

18   $1 \cdot 9$ 19 $5 \cdot 5$ 20 $10 \cdot 1$ 21 $0 \cdot 7$ 22 $13 \cdot 3$ 23 $15 \cdot 6$

35

Hundredths

Write each number as a fraction and a decimal.

1. $1\frac{26}{100} = 1\cdot26$

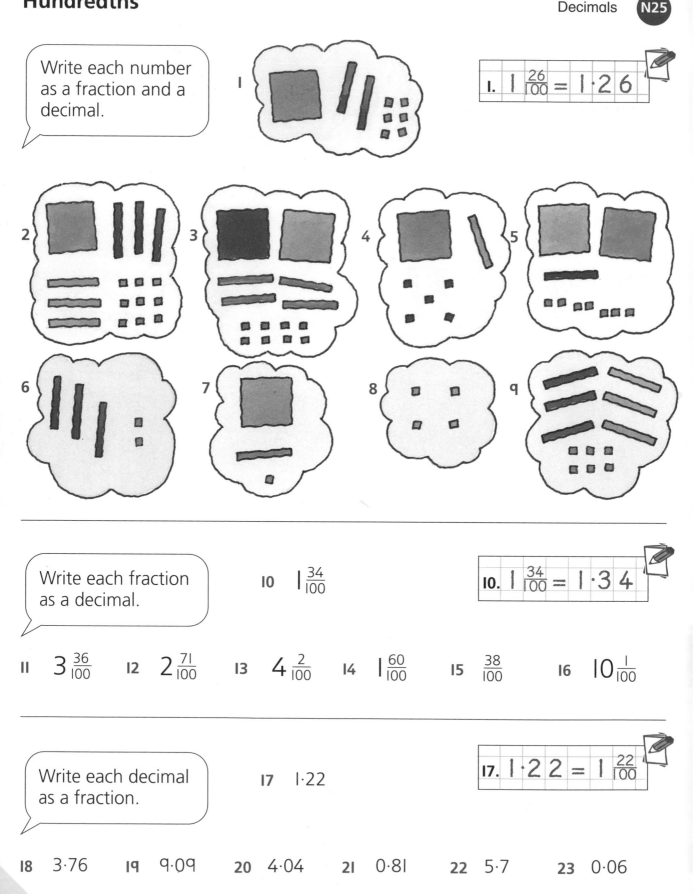

2 3 4 5

6 7 8 9

Write each fraction as a decimal.

10 $1\frac{34}{100}$

10. $1\frac{34}{100} = 1\cdot34$

11 $3\frac{36}{100}$ 12 $2\frac{71}{100}$ 13 $4\frac{2}{100}$ 14 $1\frac{60}{100}$ 15 $\frac{38}{100}$ 16 $10\frac{1}{100}$

Write each decimal as a fraction.

17 $1\cdot22$

17. $1\cdot22 = 1\frac{22}{100}$

18 $3\cdot76$ 19 $9\cdot09$ 20 $4\cdot04$ 21 $0\cdot81$ 22 $5\cdot7$ 23 $0\cdot06$

36

Tenths and hundredths

> Write how many tenths and hundredths.

1 0·71

1. $0·71 = \frac{7}{10} + \frac{1}{100}$

2 0·84   3 0·67   4 0·51   5 0·91   6 0·69

7 0·99   8 0·18   9 0·03   10 0·52   11 0·04

12 0·9   13 0·44   14 0·08   15 0·1   16 0·11

> Write each length in metres.

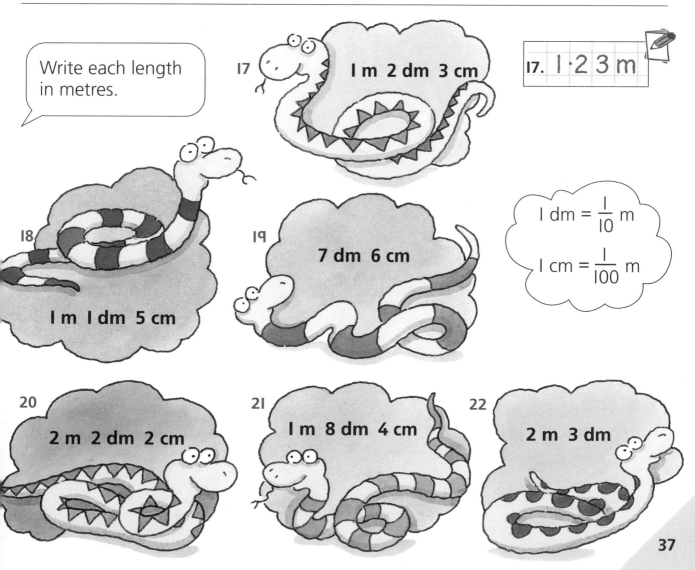

17 1 m 2 dm 3 cm

17. $1·23$ m

18 1 m 1 dm 5 cm

19 7 dm 6 cm

$1\ dm = \frac{1}{10}\ m$

$1\ cm = \frac{1}{100}\ m$

20 2 m 2 dm 2 cm

21 1 m 8 dm 4 cm

22 2 m 3 dm

37

Tenths and hundredths

Write how many litres.

1 1l 5dl 4cl

1. 1·54 l

2 3l 2dl 4cl

3 4l 8dl 9cl

4 6l 7dl 3cl

$$1 \text{ dl} = \frac{1}{10} \text{ l}$$

$$1 \text{ cl} = \frac{1}{100} \text{ l}$$

5 1l 2dl 1cl

6 2l 4dl

7 4l 6dl 4cl

8 7dl 5cl

9 1l 5dl 1cl

10 5dl 5cl

11 2l 8cl

12 5l 8dl

Write the times in order, from smallest to largest.

c. 10·01 s

Lane	Time (seconds)
A	10·1
B	10·58
C	10·01
D	10·98
E	10·23
F	10·4
G	10·04

Hundredths

Write the position of each ball.

A → 2·24 m

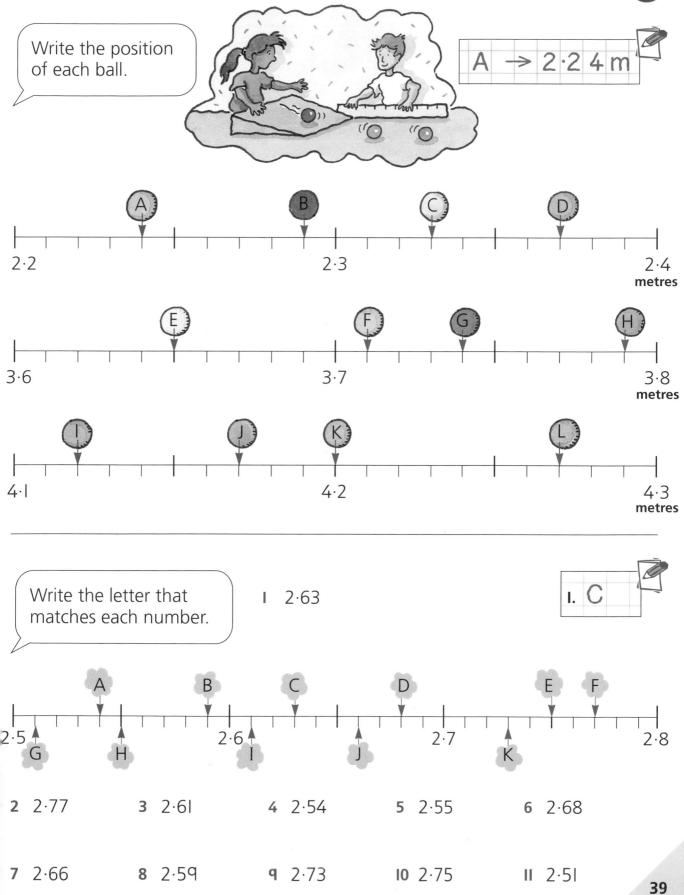

Write the letter that matches each number.

1 2·63

1. C

2 2·77   3 2·61   4 2·54   5 2·55   6 2·68

7 2·66   8 2·59   9 2·73   10 2·75   11 2·51

39

Write < or > each time.

1 1·34, 1·43

1. 1·34 < 1·43

1·3   1·4   1·5

2 1·4, 1·39   3 1·49, 1·39   4 1·31, 1·33   5 1·5, 1·49

6 1·72, 1·78   7 3·09, 3·12   8 3·48, 3·84   9 7·7, 7·8

10 10·01, 10·09   11 9·19, 9·2   12 9·07, 9·7   13 5·63, 5·66

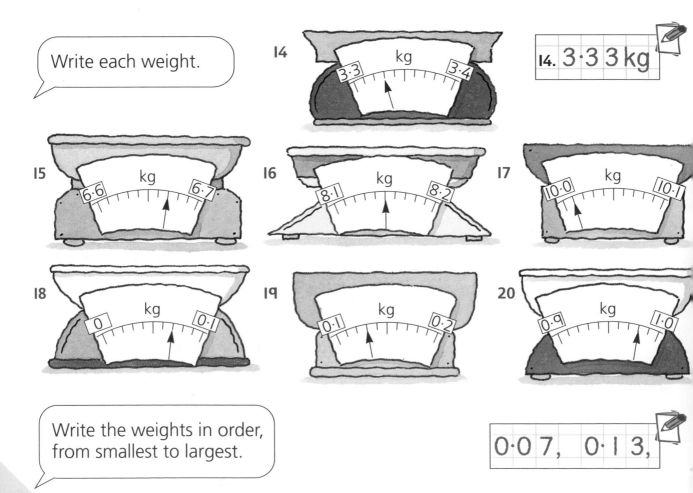

Write each weight.

14 kg 3·3 3·4

14. 3·33 kg

15 kg 6·6 6·7

16 kg 8·1 8·2

17 kg 10·0 10·1

18 kg 0 0·1

19 kg 0·1 0·2

20 kg 0·9 1·0

Write the weights in order, from smallest to largest.

0·07, 0·13,

Write the missing numbers.

1. 2·21, 2·22, 2·23

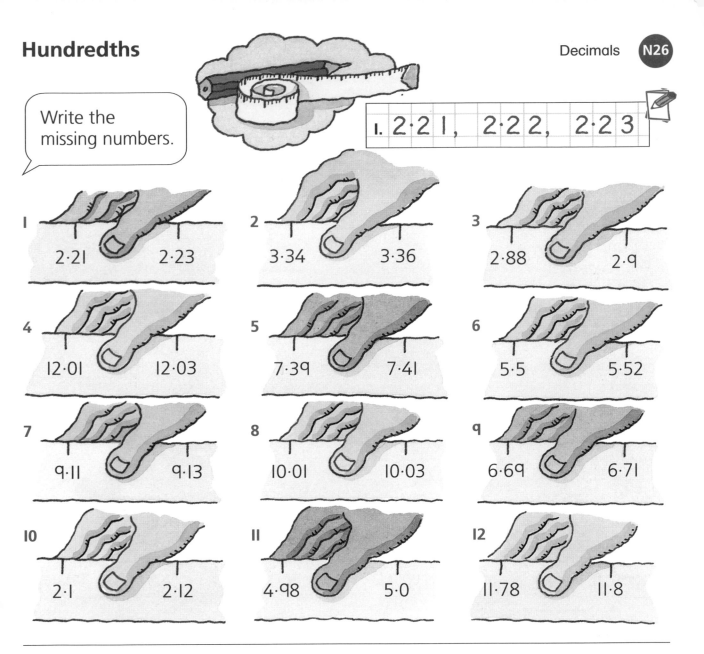

1 2·21 _____ 2·23

2 3·34 _____ 3·36

3 2·88 _____ 2·9

4 12·01 _____ 12·03

5 7·39 _____ 7·41

6 5·5 _____ 5·52

7 9·11 _____ 9·13

8 10·01 _____ 10·03

9 6·69 _____ 6·71

10 2·1 _____ 2·12

11 4·98 _____ 5·0

12 11·78 _____ 11·8

Write the times in order, from smallest to largest.

Name	Time (seconds)
Jim	56·7
Jo	56·68
Sam	56·79
Dev	56·66
Jay	56·71
Zoe	56·69
Anu	56·61
Tim	56·8
Tara	56·59
Seema	56·62

Tara, 5 6·5 9 s

Hundredths

Each price goes up by 1p.

Write the new prices.

1. £ 3·1 7

1 £3·16

2 £5·19

3 £1·19

4 £2·29

5 £3·04

6 £9·99

7 £1·99

8 £3·98

9 £8·01

10 £2·09

11 £3·23

12 £7·71

Each price goes down by 1p.

Write the new prices.

13. £ 8·8 0

13 £8·81

14 £9·98

15 £10·02

16 £7·80

17 £9·10

18 £8·00

19 £7·61

20 £4·50

21 £8·39

22 £6·48

Percentages

Write what percentage of each grid is red, blue and yellow.

1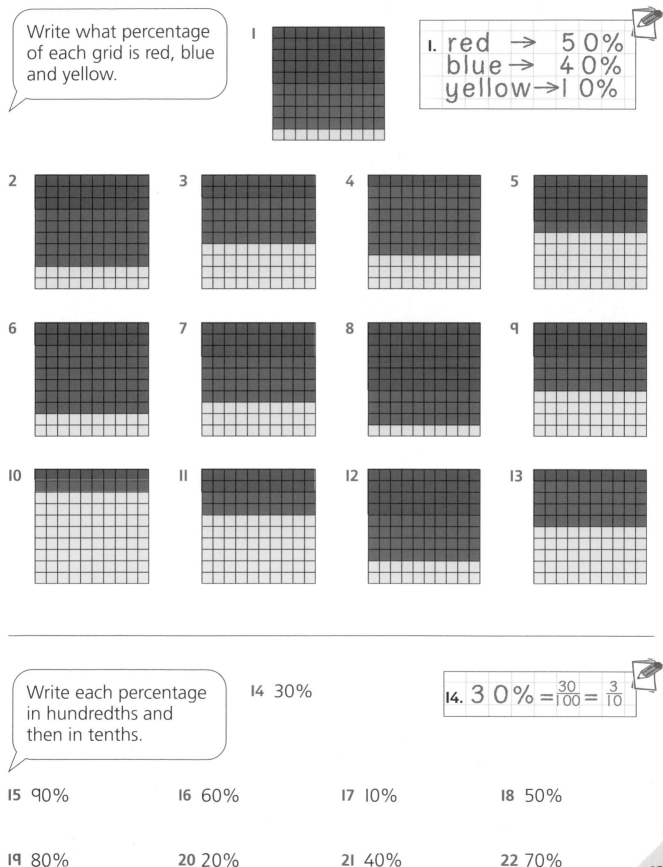

1. red → 50%
   blue → 40%
   yellow → 10%

2

3

4

5

6

7

8

9

10

11

12

13

Write each percentage in hundredths and then in tenths.

14 30%

14. $30\% = \frac{30}{100} = \frac{3}{10}$

15 90%   16 60%   17 10%   18 50%

19 80%   20 20%   21 40%   22 70%

Percentages

Write what percentage of each grid is blue.

1

1. 4 3 %

2   3   4   5

6   7   8   9

Write what percentage of each grid is yellow.

1a. 5 7 %

Write each fraction as a percentage.

10 $\frac{48}{100}$

10. 4 8 %

11 $\frac{38}{100}$ 12 $\frac{92}{100}$ 13 $\frac{40}{100}$ 14 $\frac{21}{100}$ 15 $\frac{5}{100}$

Write each percentage as a fraction.

16 29%

16. $\frac{29}{100}$

17 10%   18 98%   19 75%   20 67%   21 2%

Percentages

Draw a 10 × 10 grid.

Colour a pattern, using different colours.

Write what percentage of the grid is in each colour.

Write what percentage of each grid is green.

1. 25%

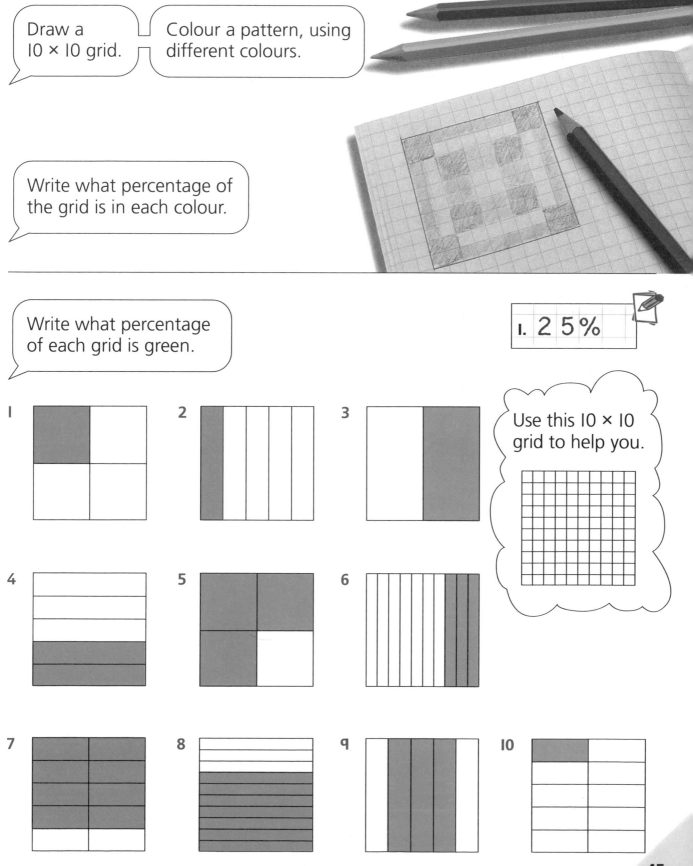

Use this 10 × 10 grid to help you.

1

2

3

4

5

6

7

8

9

10

45

Percentages

Each price goes down by 50%.

Write the new prices.

1. 5 0 % of 8 0 p = 4 0 p

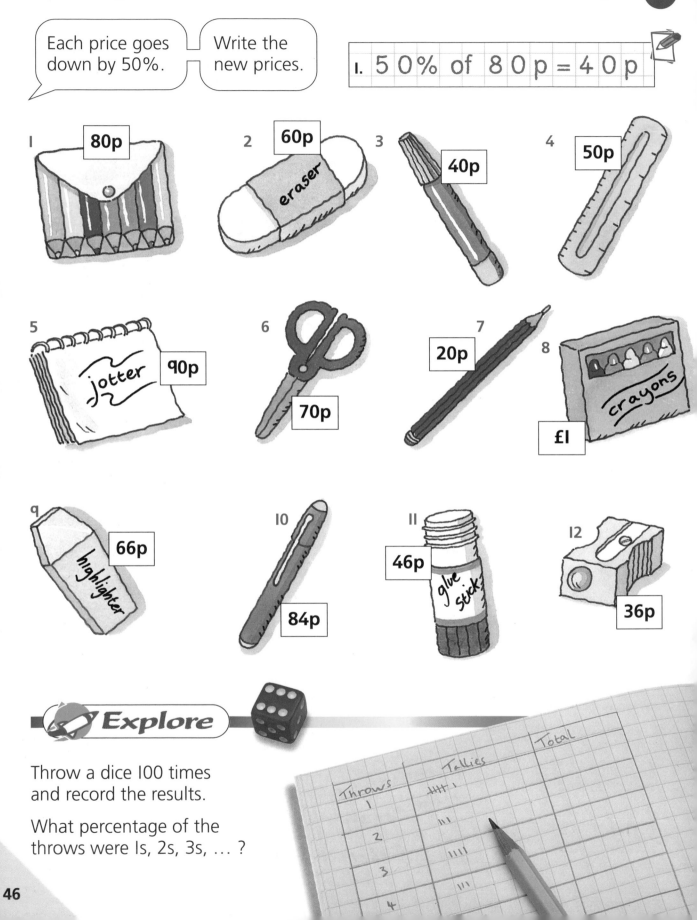

1. 80p

2. 60p

3. 40p

4. 50p

5. jotter 90p

6. 70p

7. 20p

8. crayons £1

9. highlighter 66p

10. 84p

11. glue stick 46p

12. 36p

Explore

Throw a dice 100 times and record the results.

What percentage of the throws were 1s, 2s, 3s, … ?

46

Square numbers

Write a multiplication for each set of stamps.

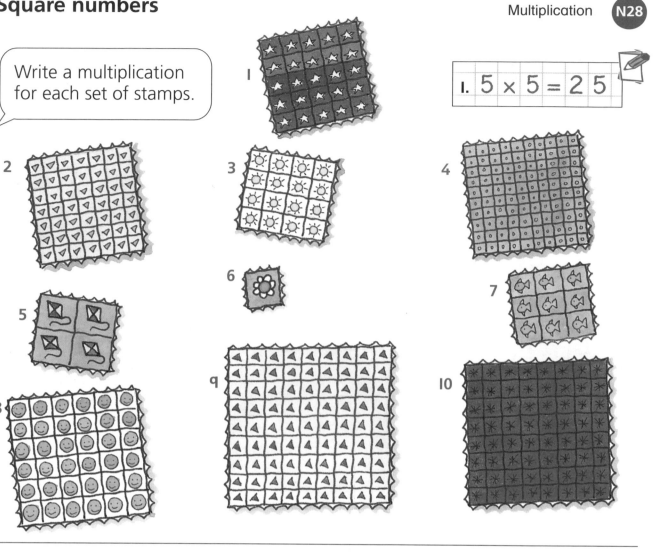

I. $5 \times 5 = 25$

Draw a square grid to match the number of stamps in each set.

II.

Square numbers

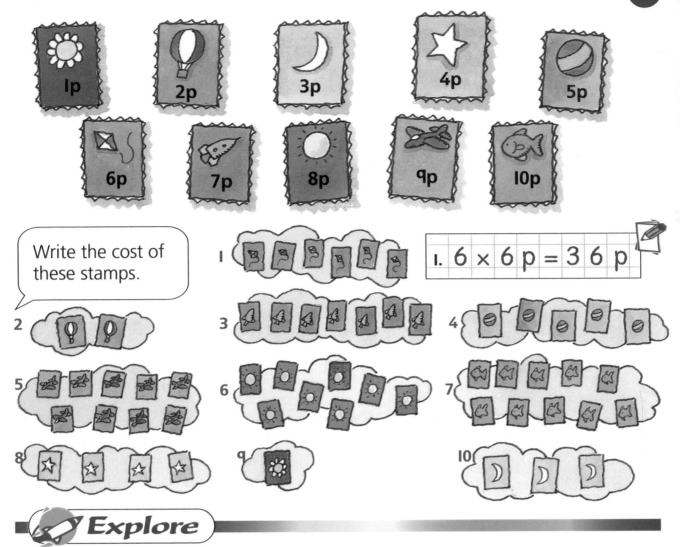

Write the cost of these stamps.

1. $6 \times 6p = 36p$

Write the units digit of each square number.

1   4   9   1 6   2 5

Describe any pattern.

Use a calculator to find the next 10 square numbers after 100.

Explore patterns in the units digit.

Explore

1	2	3	4	5	6	7	8	9	10
2	4	6	8	10	12	14	16	18	20
3	6	9	12	15	18	21	24	27	30
4	8	12	16	20	24	28	32	36	40
5	10	15	20	25	30	35	40	45	50
6	12	18	24	30	36	42	48	54	60
7	14	21	28	35	42	49	56	63	70
8	16	24	32	40	48	56	64	72	80
9	18	27	36	45	54	63	72	81	90
10	20	30	40	50	60	70	80	90	100

Square numbers

Copy the grid and write the missing numbers.

1	2	3	4	·5	6	7	8	9	10
	4	6	8	10	12	14	16	18	20
		9	12	15	18	21	24	27	30
			16	20	24	28	32	36	40
				25	30	35	40	45	50
					36	42	48	54	60
						49	56	63	70
							64	72	80
								81	90
									100

The numbers in each pair are the same.

Write the missing numbers.

1. $6 \times 6 = 36$

1 ⬡ × ⬡ = 36

2 ⬡ × ⬡ = 4

3 ⬡ × ⬡ = 81

4 ⬡ × ⬡ = 49

5 ⬡ × ⬡ = 25

6 ⬡ × ⬡ = 9

7 ⬡ × ⬡ = 100

8 ⬡ × ⬡ = 64

9 ⬡ × ⬡ = 16

Explore

Find the difference between the first 2 square numbers.

Find the difference between the second and third square numbers.

Continue. Can you see a pattern?

4 − 1 = 3

9 − 4 = 5

16 − 9 =

Multiplying

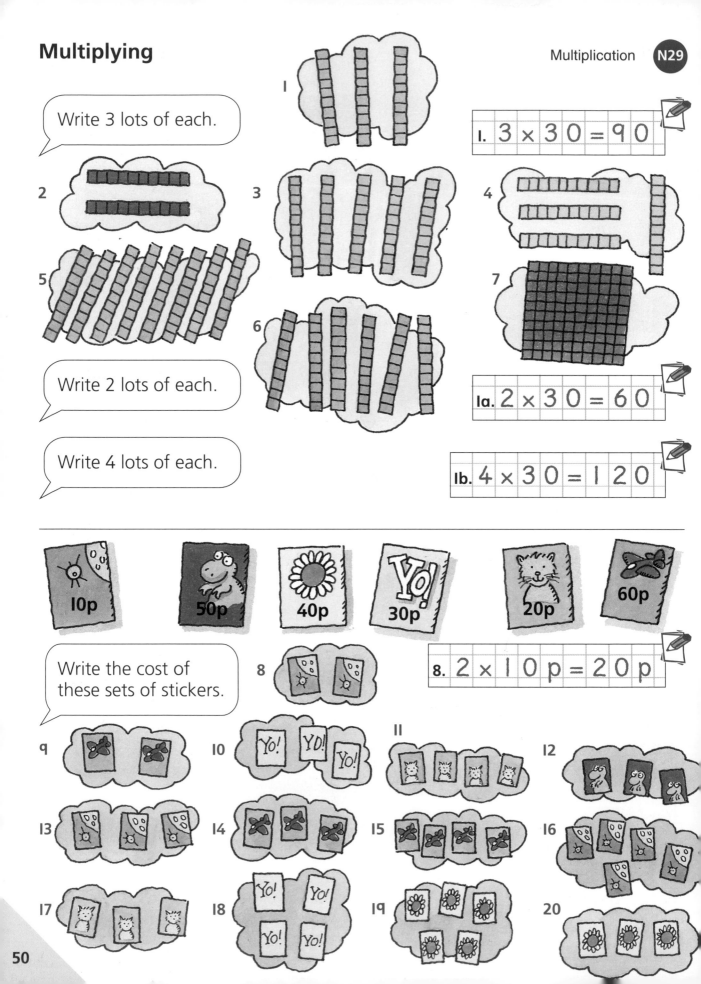

Write 3 lots of each.

1.

2

3

4

1. $3 \times 30 = 90$

Write 2 lots of each.

5

7

6

1a. $2 \times 30 = 60$

Write 4 lots of each.

1b. $4 \times 30 = 120$

10p 50p 40p 30p 20p 60p

Write the cost of these sets of stickers.

8

8. $2 \times 10p = 20p$

9   10   11   12

13   14   15   16

17   18   19   20

50

Multiplying

> Copy and complete.

1 2 × 20 =

1. $2 \times 20 = 40$

2 3 × 30 =   3 4 × 20 =   4 5 × 30 =   5 6 × 30 =

6 2 × 30 =   7 7 × 20 =   8 8 × 20 =   9 3 × 40 =

10 4 × 50 =   11 9 × 30 =   12 6 × 40 =   13 8 × 30 =

14 7 × 30 =   15 2 × 60 =   16 8 × 50 =   17 4 × 70 =

18 3 × 80 =   19 9 × 60 =   20 5 × 50 =   21 7 × 40 =

> John and Helen do lots of jobs.
>
> Write how much they earn.

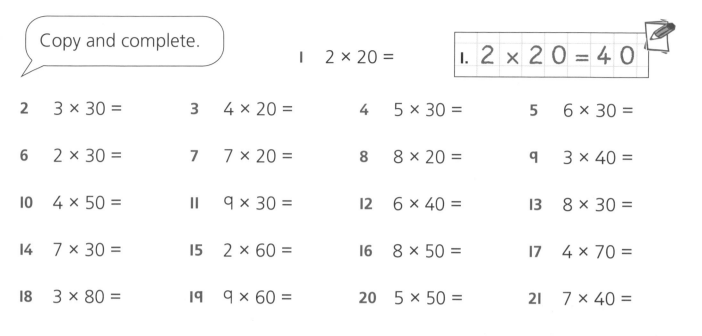

post letter 20p	wash window 50p
walk dog 40p	feed rabbit 30p
empty bin 10p	wash car 60p

22 walk 2 dogs

23 post 8 letters

22. $2 \times 40p = 80p$

24 wash 5 windows

25 feed 4 rabbits

26 wash 3 cars

27 empty 9 bins

28 wash 4 windows

29 post 5 letters

30 wash 7 cars

31 walk 4 dogs

32 empty 3 bins

51

Copy and complete the multiplication tables.

I.

×	2 0	4 0	5 0	3 0
4	8 0			
8				

1

×	20	40	50	30
4				
8				
9				

2

×	80	60	90	70
2				
3				
6				

3

×	30	40	50	60
3				
6				
9				

4

×	30	50	70	90
2				
4				
6				

Explore

Try this multiplication trick on a friend.

Give them a Ip and a 20p coin to hold, one in each hand – hidden from you!

Tell them to work out: 6 lots of the coin in their left hand, and 7 lots of the coin in their right hand.

If the total of the two answers is even, you know the Ip is in their left hand.
If it is odd, the Ip is in their right hand.

Why does this work?

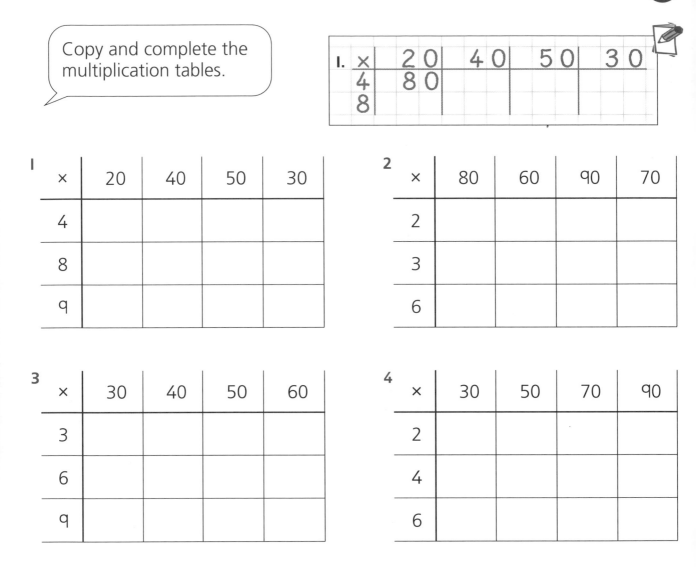

Multiplying

Copy and complete.

1.
```
    H T U
      2 7
  ×     5
```

1.
```
    H T U
      2 7
  ×     5
  ─────────
      3 5
    1 0 0
  ─────────
    1 3 5
```

2.
```
    H T U
      1 3
  ×     4
```

3.
```
    H T U
      2 1
  ×     6
```

4.
```
    H T U
      2 6
  ×     3
```

5.
```
    H T U
      3 2
  ×     4
```

6.
```
    H T U
      1 5
  ×     5
```

7.
```
    H T U
      4 3
  ×     4
```

8.
```
    H T U
      5 2
  ×     3
```

9.
```
    H T U
      3 8
  ×     5
```

10.
```
    H T U
      6 4
  ×     3
```

11.
```
    H T U
      3 4
  ×     7
```

12.
```
    H T U
      4 5
  ×     6
```

The children are seated in rows.

Write how many in total.

13. 4 rows of 22

13.
```
    H T U
      2 2
  ×     4
  ─────────
        8
    8 0
  ─────────
    8 8
```

14. 3 rows of 15

15. 2 rows of 24

16. 4 rows of 32

17. 5 rows of 27

18. 3 rows of 35

19. 3 rows of 17

20. 2 rows of 41

21. 4 rows of 23

22. 5 rows of 29

23. 6 rows of 38

24. 7 rows of 45

25. 4 rows of 64

Multiplying

Write how many sweets in total.

1

24 sweets in a box
4 boxes

	H	T	U
1.		2	4
×			4
	1	6	
	8	0	
	9	6	

2
28 sweets
in a box
3 boxes

3
25 sweets
in a box
5 boxes

4
16 sweets
in a box
6 boxes

5
14 sweets
in a box
7 boxes

6
32 sweets
in a box
5 boxes

7
21 sweets
in a box
4 boxes

8
18 sweets
in box
4 boxes

9
12 sweets
in a box
6 boxes

10
22 sweets
in a box
3 boxes

11
40 sweets
in a box
4 boxes

12
36 sweets
in a box
5 boxes

13
17 sweets
in a box
6 boxes

Copy and complete the multiplication table.

×	29	35	42	19
3	87			
4				
6				
8				

	H	T	U
14.		2	9
×			3
		2	7
	6	0	
	8	7	

54

Multiplying

grapefruit 3Ip each

oranges 26p each

apples 14p each

pears 18p each

coconuts 42p each

Write the total cost of:

I. 5 grapefruit

2. 4 oranges

3. 5 pears

4. 7 coconuts

5. 8 apples

6. 6 oranges

7. 4 grapefruit

8. 4 coconuts

I.
	H	T	U	
		3	I	
×			5	
			5	
	I	5	0	
	I	5	5	p

2Ip each

13p each

34p each

27p each

4Ip each

q. 6 sharpeners

Write the total cost of:

10. 5 rubbers

11. 6 pens

12. 4 rulers

13. 6 pencils

14. 7 rubbers

15. 3 sharpeners

16. 8 pens

q.
	H	T	U	
		I	3	
×			6	
		I	8	
		6	0	
		7	8	p

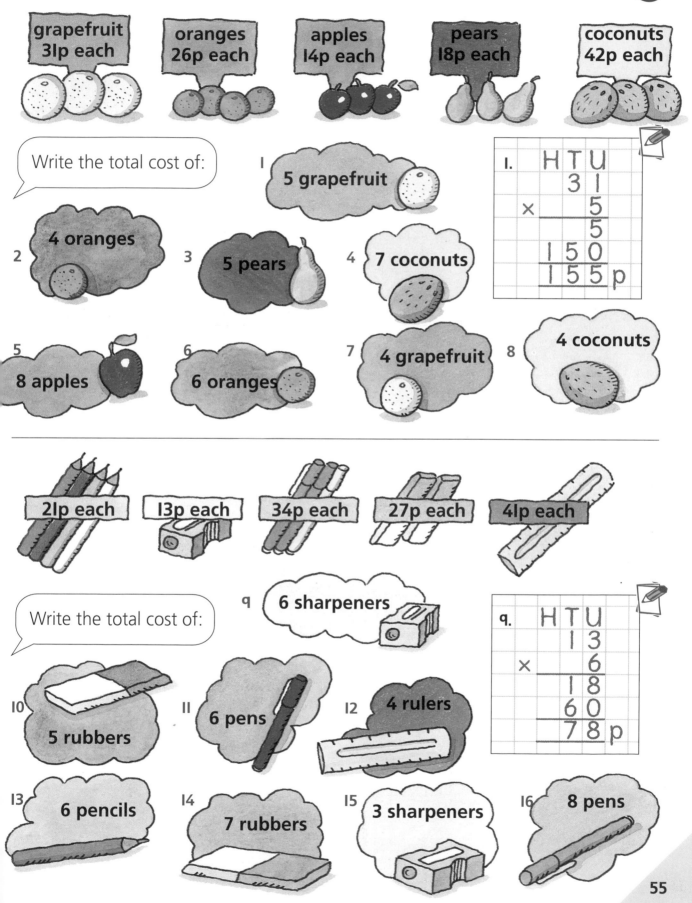

55

Write the perimeter of each swimming pool.

1

←23 m→

	H	T	U
1.		2	3
×			4
	1	2	
	8	0	
	9	2	m

2

←18 m→

3

16 m

4

←22 m→

5

←29 m→

6

←14 m→

7

←32 m→

8

←33 m→

9

45 m

Explore

Use number cards 2, 3, 4, 5.

Arrange any 3 to make a multiplication.

What are the largest and smallest possible answers?

How many different answers can you find?

2 3 4

H	T	U
	2	3
		4
×	1	2
	8	0
	9	2

Dividing

Copy and complete.

1   2)80

I.   40
    2)80

2   3)60   3   2)40   4   2)20   5   3)90   6   4)40

7   3)30   8   2)60   9   4)80   10 6)120   11 5)100

These children are going on a train journey.

Write how many groups go on each journey.

12.   1 2
     4)4 8

12   48 children sit in 4s

13   24 children sit in 2s

14   39 children sit in 3s

15   33 children sit in 3s

16   36 children sit in 3s

17   28 children sit in 2s

18   69 children sit in 3s

19   46 children sit in 2s

20   44 children sit in 4s

Dividing

Copy and complete.

1 $2\overline{)14}$

1. $2\overline{)1\ 4}$ with 7 above

2 $3\overline{)18}$

3 $5\overline{)25}$

4 $4\overline{)36}$

5 $4\overline{)24}$

6 $6\overline{)36}$

7 $2\overline{)12}$

8 $4\overline{)32}$

9 $6\overline{)48}$

10 $5\overline{)35}$

11 $3\overline{)24}$

The balls are packed in different boxes.

Write how many boxes for each set.

12. $3\overline{)2\ 7}$ with 9 above

12 27 balls
3 in a box

13 20 balls
4 in a box

14 16 balls
2 in a box

15 45 balls
5 in a box

16 42 balls
6 in a box

17 28 balls
4 in a box

18 21 balls
3 in a box

19 18 balls
2 in a box

20 54 balls
6 in a box

21 72 balls
6 in a box

22 42 balls
3 in a box

23 52 balls
4 in a box

Dividing

Copy and complete.

1 2)69

I.   3 4 r 1
     2)6 9

2 3)94   3 4)86   4 2)47   5 3)61   6 5)57

7 3)98   8 4)49   9 3)35   10 2)85   11 5)52

The batteries fit different torches.

Write how many torches for each set.

Write how many batteries are left over.

12
49 batteries
4 in a torch

13
32 batteries
3 in a torch

12. 1 2 r 1
     4)4 9

14
62 batteries
6 in a torch

15
82 batteries
4 in a torch

16
34 batteries
3 in a torch

17
64 batteries
3 in a torch

18
43 batteries
4 in a torch

19
67 batteries
6 in a torch

20
38 batteries
3 in a torch

21
41 batteries
2 in a torch

22
68 batteries
3 in a torch

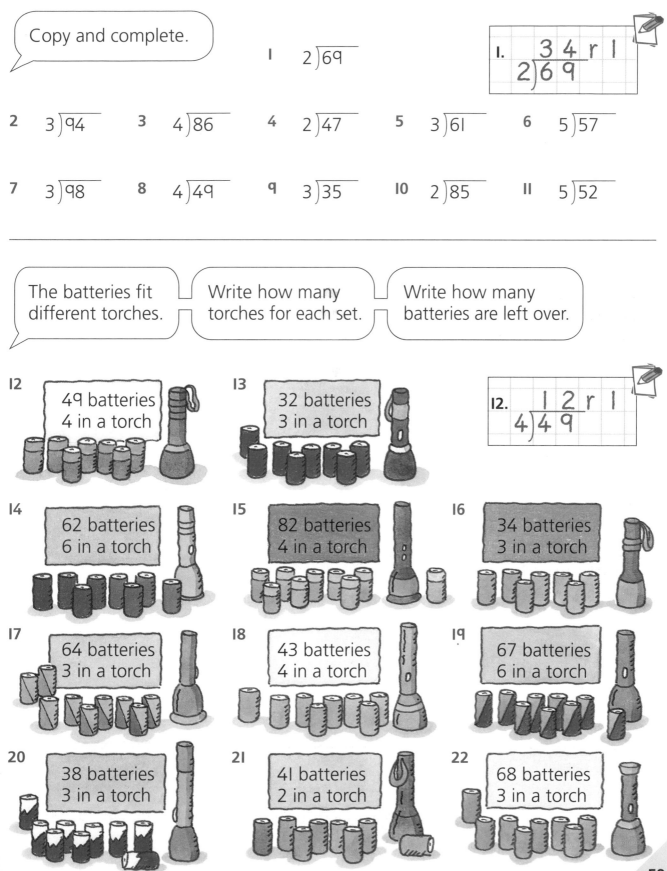

The chocolate bars are packed in different boxes.

Write how many boxes for each set.

Write how many bars left over.

1
73 bars
6 in a box

2
66 bars
4 in a box

1.
```
    1 2 r 1
6)7¹3
```

3
81 bars
7 in a box

4
47 bars
3 in a box

5
58 bars
4 in a box

6
62 bars
5 in a box

7
54 bars
4 in a box

8
72 bars
5 in a box

9
95 bars
6 in a box

10
74 bars
4 in a box

11
82 bars
6 in a box

Explore

Which number between 50 and 100 leaves a remainder of 1 when divided by: 2, 3, 4, 5, 6?

```
  2 5
2)5¹0

  2 5 r1
2)5¹1

  1 7
3)5²3
```

Dividing

Copy and complete.

I 3)600

I. $\begin{array}{r} 2\,0\,0 \\ 3\overline{)6\,0\,0} \end{array}$

2 2)600   3 3)300   4 2)200   5 4)800   6 2)400

7 4)400   8 5)500   9 2)800   10 6)600   11 3)900

12 3)690   13 4)480   14 2)640   15 3)360   16 4)840

17 4)440   18 2)280   19 2)420   20 3)930   21 5)550

The bottles are packed in different boxes.

Write how many boxes for each set.

22. $\begin{array}{r} 1\,1\,0 \\ 3\overline{)3\,3\,0} \end{array}$

22 330 bottles
3 in a box

23 680 bottles
2 in a box

24 390 bottles
3 in a box

25 660 bottles
6 in a box

26 880 bottles
4 in a box

27 630 bottles
3 in a box

28 960 bottles
3 in a box

29 660 bottles
3 in a box

30 840 bottles
2 in a box

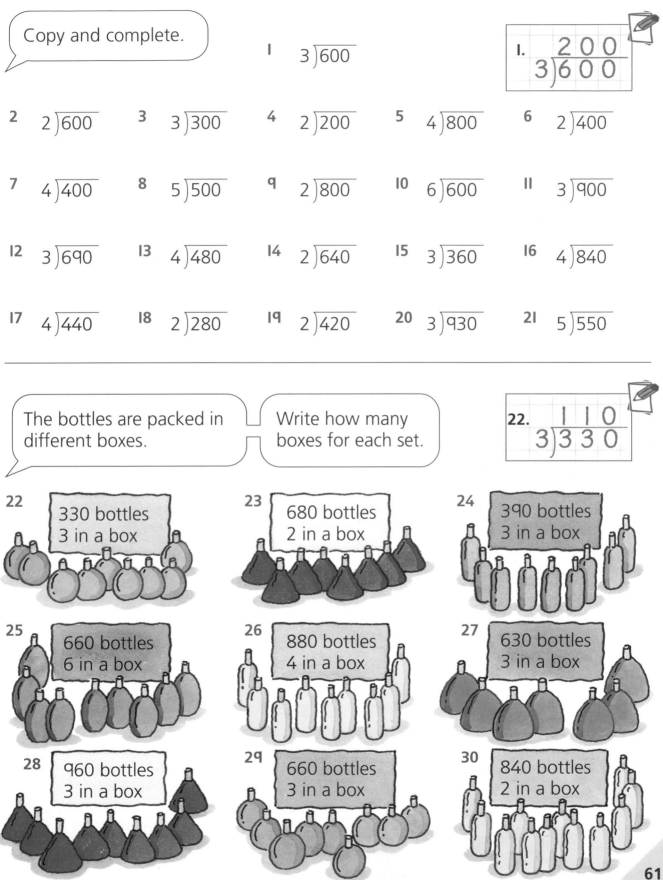

Dividing

Copy and complete.

I   3)696

I.
```
      2 3 2
   3) 6 9 6
```

2   4)848

3   3)369

4   4)484

5   2)482

6   4)844

7   2)624

8   3)936

9   3)336

10   4)448

11   3)633

The cakes are packed in different boxes.

Write how many boxes for each set.

12.
```
      1 3 1
   4) 5 ¹2 4
```

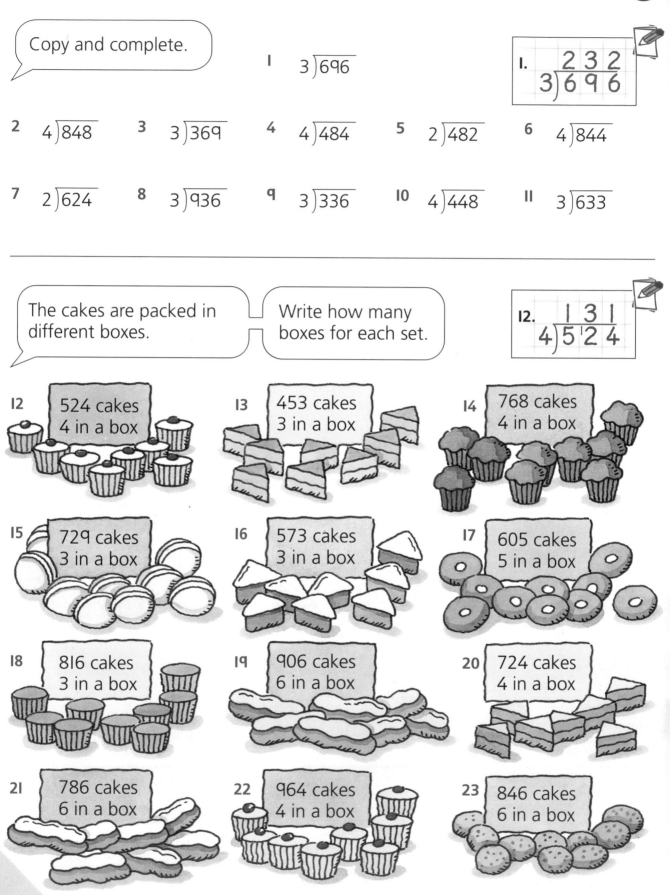

12   524 cakes 4 in a box

13   453 cakes 3 in a box

14   768 cakes 4 in a box

15   729 cakes 3 in a box

16   573 cakes 3 in a box

17   605 cakes 5 in a box

18   816 cakes 3 in a box

19   906 cakes 6 in a box

20   724 cakes 4 in a box

21   786 cakes 6 in a box

22   964 cakes 4 in a box

23   846 cakes 6 in a box

Dividing

Copy and complete.

1 3)348

I.
```
    1 1 6
3) 3 4 ⁱ8
```

2 5)565   3 3)675   4 4)464   5 4)492   6 6)696

7 6)684   8 4)456   9 3)381   10 3)687   11 4)896

12 4)548   13 3)537   14 5)725   15 4)612   16 3)825

17 6)864   18 3)462   19 4)756   20 7)875   21 6)978

The pies are packed in different boxes.

Write how many boxes for each set.

22.
```
     2 4 7
3) 7 ⁱ4 ²1
```

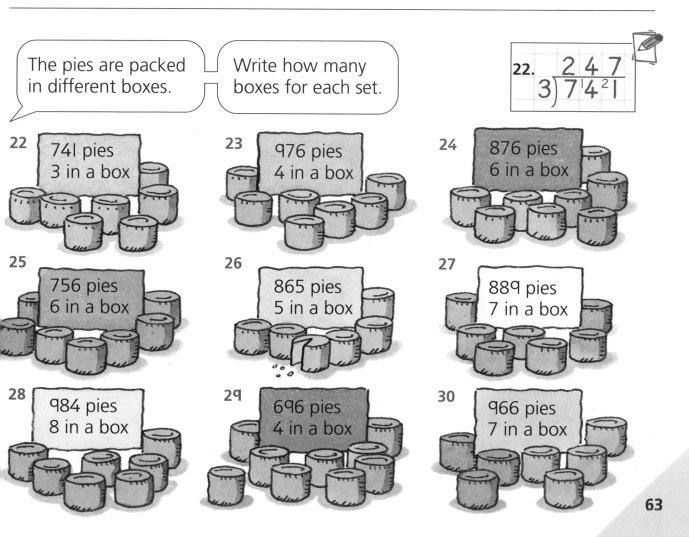

22 741 pies
3 in a box

23 976 pies
4 in a box

24 876 pies
6 in a box

25 756 pies
6 in a box

26 865 pies
5 in a box

27 889 pies
7 in a box

28 984 pies
8 in a box

29 696 pies
4 in a box

30 966 pies
7 in a box

Dividing

Copy and complete.

1 3)695

1. 2 3 1 r 2
    3)6 9 5

2 2)487   3 3)364   4 4)486   5 5)558   6 4)445

7 2)685   8 4)849   9 3)392   10 2)261   11 4)483

12 3)542   13 2)543   14 6)789   15 4)926   16 4)643

17 5)758   18 4)565   19 3)755   20 6)964   21 3)874

The pens are put in different packs.

Write how many packs for each set.

Write how many pens left over.

22 878 pens
    6 in a pack

23 673 pens
    5 in a pack

22. 1 4 6 r 2
     6)8 ²7 ³8

24 922 pens
    6 in a pack

25 657 pens
    4 in a pack

26 954 pens
    7 in a pack

27 946 pens
    4 in a pack

28 863 pens
    7 in a pack

29 768 pens
    5 in a pack